Merriam-Webster's Vocabulary Builder

Review Quizzes

Second Edition

Mary Wood Cornog

Merriam-Webster, Incorporated
Springfield, Massachusetts

A GENUINE MERRIAM-WEBSTER

The name Webster alone is no guarantee of excellence. It is used by a number of publishers and may serve mainly to mislead an unwary buyer.
Merriam-Webster™ is the name you should look for when you consider the purchase of dictionaries or other fine reference books. It carries the reputation of a company that has been publishing since 1831 and is your assurance of quality and authority.

Merriam-Webster's Vocabulary Builder, Second Edition.

Copyright © 2020 Concerto Publishing

미리엄웹스터 보캐뷸러리빌더 부록으로 제공하는 이 워크북은 유닛마다 공부한 단어를 얼마나 기억하고 있는지 테스트하기 위한 리뷰퀴즈를 제공한다.

단어와 가장 의미가 가장 가까운 단어를 찾는 문제, 비슷한말과 반댓말을 찾는 문제, 문장의 빈칸을 채우는 문제 등 대부분 익숙한 문제들로 구성되어 있다.

하지만 유추(analogy) 퀴즈는 다소 생소하게 느껴질 수도 있다. 어려워할 필요는 없다. 첫 두 단어 사이의 관계와 같은 관계를 갖는 단어를 찾아내면 된다.

실제 문제를 보자.

calculate: count :: expend: _____

a. stretch b. speculate c. pay d. explode

이 문제를 풀어서 설명하자면 'calculate 와 count 의 관계는 expend 와 _____의 관계와 같다'는 뜻이다. 빈 칸에는 어떤 단어가 들어가야 할까? 아래 나와있는 네 단어 중에서 하나를 고르면 된다. calculate 와 count 는 비슷한 말이므로, expend 와 비슷한 말을 찾으면 된다.

정답은 pay 다.

Unit 1

A. Choose the closest definition:

1. impotent   a. antique   b. weak   c. broken   d. skimpy
2. deplete   a. straighten out   b. draw down   c. fold   d. abandon
3. stentorian   a. obnoxious   b. muffled   c. loud   d. dictated
4. potentate   a. ruler   b. bully   c. warrior   d. prime minister
5. plenipotentiary   a. monarch   b. ambassador   c. fullness   d. likely possibility
6. protean   a. meaty   b. powerful   c. changeable   d. professional
7. potential   a. privilege   b. prestige   c. power   d. possibility
8. complement   a. praise   b. number required   c. abundance   d. usual dress
9. plenary   a. for hours   b. for life   c. for officials   d. for everyone
10. replete   a. refold   b. repeat   c. abundantly provided   d. fully clothed
11. nestor   a. journalist   b. long-winded elder   c. domestic hen   d. judge

B. Match the definition on the left to the correct word on the right:

1. replete   a.   drain
2. deplete   b.   brimming
3. plenary   c.   counterpart
4. complement   d.   general

C. Complete the analogy:

1. amount : quantity :: complement ____
   a. remainder   b. extra   c. extension   d. minority
2. strong : vigorous :: impotent : ____
   a. healthy   b. fragile   c. powerful   d. weak

D. Indicate whether the pairs have the same or different meanings:

1. animosity / hatred   same ___ / different ___
2. potentate / monarch   same ___ / different ___
3. magnanimous / petty   same ___ / different ___
4. plenipotentiary / emperor   same ___ / different ___
5. animated / lively   same ___ / different ___
6. impotent / powerless   same ___ / different ___
7. inanimate / not alive   same ___ / different ___
8. potential / influence   same ___ / different ___

E. Choose the correct synonym and the correct antonym:

1. animated   a. colorful   b. lifeless   c. smiling   d. vigorous
2. Achilles' heel   a. paradise   b. heroism   c. strong point   d. vulnerability
3. Animosity   a. affection   b. mammal   c. dedication   d. hatred

F. Match each word on the left to its *antonym* on the right:

1. deplete   a. empty
2. replete   b. fill

G. Fill in each blank with the correct letter:

a. complement   d. animated   g. protean
b. inanimate   e. potentate   h. animosity
c. stentorian   f. magnanimous   i. Achilles' heel

1. Actors like Robin Williams seem ＿＿ in their ability to assume different characters.
2. He holds court in his vast 15th-floor office like an oriental ＿＿, signing documents and issuing commands.
3. Inviting her former rival to take part in the conference was a ＿＿ gesture.
4. The judge was known for issuing all his rulings in a ＿＿ voice.
5. The ＿＿ form of the dog lay stretched in front of the fire for hours.
6. Another ＿＿ discussion about politics was going on when they arrived at the bar that evening.
7. The best negotiators always make a serious study of the basic causes of the ＿＿ between feuding partners.
8. Believing the flattery of others and enjoying the trappings of power have often been the ＿＿ of successful politicians.
9. Fresh, hot bread is the perfect ＿＿ to any dinner.

UNIT 2

A. Choose the closest definition:

1. matriarch   a. goddess   b. mermaid   c. bride   d. grande dame
2. patrician   a. patriot   b. aristocrat   c. father   d. grandfather
3. ascendancy   a. growth   b. climb   c. dominance   d. rank
4. descendant   a. offspring   b. ancestor   c. cousin   d. forerunner
5. matrix   a. formula   b. alternate reality   c. scheme   d. source
6. transcend   a. exceed   b. astound   c. fulfill   d. transform
7. mentor   a. translator   b. interpreter   c. guide   d. student
8. condescend   a. stoop   b. remove   c. agree   d. reject
9. maternity   a. motherhood   b. nightgown   c. women's club   d. marriage
10. matrilineal   a. through the mother's family   b. graduating
              c. adopted   d. female

B. Match the definition on the left to the correct word on the right:

1.	paternalistic	a.	domination
2.	matrilineal	b.	through the mother's line
3.	patriarchy	c.	exercising fatherly authority
4.	ascendancy	d.	aristocrat
5.	patrician	e.	person living abroad
6.	expatriate	f.	humiliating

C. Fill in each blank with the correct letter:

a. ascendancy	e. maternity	i. paternalistic
b. condescend	f. matriarch	j. patriarchy
c. descendant	g. matrilineal	k. patrician
d. expatriate	h. matrix	l. transcend

1. His family and upbringing were ___, but he still considered himself a man of the people.
2. He'd been married to Cynthia for three years, but she hadn't yet dared to introduce him to her great-aunt, the family ___.
3. She lives in a very glamorous world these days, and she would never ___ to show up at a family reunion.
4. The tribe seemed to be ___, with all inheritances passing through the females rather than the males.
5. The country could still be called a ___, with men being completely dominant both at home and in the government.
6. She'll remind you that she's a ___ of some fairly famous people, but she won't mention that the family also has some criminals in its past.
7. The Democrats are in the ___ at the moment, but they may not be next year.
8. At Christian colleges, policies tend to be rather strict and ___.
9. After five years living in the suburb, they felt they had become part of a complex social ___.
10. She soon realized that she wasn"t the only American ___ in her Kenyan village.
11. These made-for-TV movies are made for very little money and almost never ___ the lowest level of acting and production.
12. Marriage didn't seem to affect her much, but ___ has changed her completely.

D. Complete the analogy:

1. baby : mother :: descendant : ___
   a. brother   b. offspring   c. child   d. ancestor

E. Indicate whether the pairs have the same or different meanings:

1.	odyssey / journey	same ___ / different ___
2.	siren / temptress	same ___ / different ___
3.	matrix / puzzle	same ___ / different ___

F. Choose the word that does not belong:

1. maternity   a. femininity b. parenthood c. motherliness d. motherhood

G. Fill in each blank with the correct letter:

a. condescend   d. odyssey   g. Penelope
b. expatriate   e. transcend   h. Siren
c. mentor   f. paternalistic

1. He's one of the few people in the office who manages to ____ all the unpleasantness that goes on around here.
2. She was a ____ of the screen in the 1920s, luring men to their doom in movie after movie.
3. He soon discovered that he wasn't the only American ____ living in the Guatemalan village.
4. While he was away on maneuvers, his wife stayed loyally at home like a true ____.
5. The company's ____ attitudes toward its employees were at times helpful and at times just irritating.
6. He invites his wife's family to their place on holidays, but he would never ____ to go to their house instead.
7. The company president took the new recruit under her wing and acted as her ____ for the next several years.
8. On their four-month ____ they visited most of the major cities of Asia.

UNIT 3

A. Choose the closest definition:

1. exculpate   a. convict b. prove innocent c. suspect d. prove absent
2. decriminalize   a. discriminate b. legalize c. legislate d. decree
3. mea culpa   a. rejection b. apology c. excuse d. forgiveness
4. criminology   a. crime history b. crime book
                    c. crime study d. crime story
5. culpable   a. disposable b. refundable c. guilty d. harmless
6. inculpate   a. incorporate b. resist c. accuse d. offend

B. Complete the analogy:

1. fine : speeding :: penance : ____
   a. misdeed b. credit card c. fee d. behavior
2. educational : school :: penal : ____
   a. judge b. police c. prison d. sentence

3. encouraging : reward :: punitive : ___
   a. damage b. penalty c. praise d. jury
4. immunity : sickness :: impunity : ___
   a. death b. flood c. punishment d. sleep

C. Match the definition on the left to the correct word on the right:

1.	accuse	a.	criminology
2.	study of illegal behavior	b.	recrimination
3.	penal	c.	mea culpa
4.	reduce penalty for	d.	culpable
5.	blamable	e.	disciplinary
6.	confession	f.	exculpate
7.	counterattack	g.	decriminalize
8.	excuse	h.	penance

D. Choose the word that does not belong:

1.	lethargic	a. lazy b. sluggish c. energetic d. indifferent
2.	Hades	a. underworld b. heaven c. dead d. eternity
3.	stygian	a. glamorous b. gloomy c. grim d. dank
4.	punitive	a. disciplinary b. punishing c. correctional d. encouraging
5.	culpable	a. prisonlike b. misleading c. guilty d. innocent

E. Fill in each blank with the correct letter:

a. impunity	d. inculpate	g. exculpate
b. incriminate	e. Elysium	h. penance
c. punitive	f. penal	

1. You can't go on breaking the speed limit with ___ forever.
2. In trying to ___ herself, she only made herself look guiltier.
3. She spoke about her country place as an ___ where they could spend their lives surrounded by beauty.
4. The mildest of the federal ___ institutions are the so-called "country club" prisons.
5. In some households, grounding is a severe form of ___ action.
6. As ___ during the period of Lent, Christians may give up a favorite food.
7. Who would have guessed that it would take the killer's own daughter to ___ him.
8. He's trying hard to ___ as many of his friends in the crime as he can.

F. Indicate whether the pairs have the same or different meanings:

1.	decriminalize / tolerate	same ___ / different ___
2.	penance / regret	same ___ / different ___
3.	criminology / murder	same ___ / different ___
4.	penal / legal	same ___ / different ___
5.	incriminate / acquit	same ___ / different ___

6. impunity / freedom from harm   same ___ / different ___
7. recrimination / faultfinding   same ___ / different ___
8. lethargic / energetic   same ___ / different ___

UNIT 4

A. Complete the analogy:

1. initial : beginning :: irrevocable : ___
    a. usual b. noisy c. final d. reversible
2. piano : nightclub :: calliope : ___
    a. organ b. circus c. church d. steam
3. reject : accept :: equivocate : ___
    a. decide b. specify c. detect d. delay
4. melodic : notes :: phonetic : ___
    a. sounds b. signs c. ideas d. pages
5. prefer : dislike :: advocate : ___
    a. oppose b. support c. assist d. boost
6. arithmetic : numbers :: phonics : ___
    a. letters b. notes c. meanings d. music
7. multistoried : floor :: polyphonic : ___
    a. poetry b. melody c. story d. harmony
8. rodent : woodchuck :: primate : ___
    a. zoology b. mammal c. antelope d. baboon
9. monotonous : boring :: vociferous : ___
    a. vegetarian b. angry c. favorable d. noisy
10. stillness : quiet :: cacophony : ___
    a. melodious b. dissonant c. creative d. birdlike

B. Fill in each blank with the correct letter:

a. primer	e. muse	i. paean
b. equivocate	f. primordial	j. a fortiori
c. primate	g. mnemonic	
d. cacophony	h. primal	

1. Since they earned high honors for achieving a 3.7 average, ___ we should do so for getting a 3.8.
2. At her 40th birthday party, her best friend delivered a glowing ___ that left her in tears.
3. She always learns her students' names quickly by using her own ___ devices.

4. We opened the door onto a haze of cigarette smoke and a ____ of music and laughter.
5. All the ____ species look after their children for much longer than almost any other mammals.
6. After his last book of poetry was published, his ____ seemed to have abandoned him.
7. They were charmed by the ____ innocence of the little village.
8. Whenever they asked for a definite date, he would ____ and try to change the subject.
9. The asteroids in our solar system may be remnants of a ____ cloud of dust.
10. The only language instruction the child had ever gotten was from a basic ____, but he was already reading at the fifth-grade level.

C. Choose the closest definition:
1. phonetic   a. called b. twitched c. sounded d. remembered
2. cacophony   a. fraud b. argument c. racket d. panic
3. muse   a. singer b. poetry c. inspiration d. philosopher
4. polyphonic   a. multi-melodic b. uniformly harmonic
                   c. relatively boring d. musically varied

D. Choose the correct synonym and the correct antonym:
1. irrevocable   a. final b. undoable c. unbelievable d. vocal
2. vociferous   a. speechless b. steely c. sweet-sounding d. loud
3. equivocate   a. equalize b. dither c. decide d. enjoy

E. Indicate whether the pairs have the same or different meanings:
1. primal / first   same ___ / different ___
2. advocate / describe   same ___ / different ___
3. phonetic / phonelike   same ___ / different ___
4. primate / ape-family member   same ___ / different ___
5. equivocate / refuse   same ___ / different ___
6. phonics / audio   same ___ / different ___
7. primordial / primitive   same ___ / different ___
8. irrevocable / unfortunate   same ___ / different ___
9. primer / firstborn   same ___ / different ___
10. polyphonic / many-voiced   same ___ / different ___
11. cacophony / din   same ___ / different ___
12. mnemonic / ideal   same ___ / different ___
13. vociferous / calm   same ___ / different ___
14. primal / highest   same ___ / different ___

UNIT 5

A. Choose the closest definition:

1. portfolio   a. mushroom   b. folder   c. painting   d. carriage
2. deportment   a. manner   b. section   c. departure   d. promotion
3. portage   a. small dock   b. river obstacle   c. light boat   d. short carry
4. comport   a. bend   b. behave   c. join   d. transport
5. perjury   a. suing   b. cursing   c. misleading   d. lying
6. factotum   a. computer printout   b. carved pole   c. plumber   d. assistant

B. Match the definition on the left to the correct word on the right:

1.	weakening	a.	interject
2.	depression	b.	defamation
3.	expectation	c.	trajectory
4.	slander	d.	debase
5.	disgrace	e.	degenerative
6.	behave	f.	conjecture
7.	curved path	g.	dejection
8.	interrupt with	h.	projection
9.	assume	i.	comport

C. Fill in each blank with the correct letter:

a. portage   d. degenerative   g. comport
b. debase   e. portfolio   h. dejection
c. deportment   f. defamation

1. She's bringing suit against her former husband for ___, claiming that statements he had made to a reporter had caused her to lose her job.
2. Their ___ consisted mostly of high-tech stocks.
3. Dogs often suffer from ___ joint diseases that get worse year by year.
4. The biggest challenge would be the half-mile ___ around the river's worst rapids.
5. His ___ after getting turned down by his top two colleges was so deep that he didn't smile for weeks.
6. She never fails to impress people with her elegant ___ in the most difficult social situations.
7. Her friends all told her that a star like her would just ___ herself by appearing in TV ads.
8. These figures don't ___ with the ones you showed us yesterday.

D. Indicate whether the pairs have the same or different meanings:

1. degenerative / corrupt   same ___ / different ___
2. dejection / sadness   same ___ / different ___
3. deportment / behavior   same ___ / different ___
4. devalue / debase   same ___ / different ___

5. conjecture / guess   same ___ / different ___
6. primordial / existing from the beginning   same ___ / different ___

E. Choose the odd word:

1. conjecture   a. suppose b. assume c. guess d. know
2. projection   a. survey b. forecast c. report d. history
3. trajectory   a. curve b. path c. arc d. target
4. interject   a. insert b. grab c. add ` stick in

F. Choose the correct synonym and the correct antonym:

1. Dionysian   a. frenzied b. angry c. calm d. fatal
2. apollonian   a. fruity b. irrational c. single d. harmonious
3. bacchanalian   a. restrained b. dynamic c. frenzied d. forthright

G. Fill in each blank with the correct letter:

     a. defamation   d. bacchanalian   g. trajectory
     b. comport   e. satyr
     c. interject   f. deportment

1. She describes her uncle as a ___, who behaves outrageously around every young woman he meets at a party.
2. Her impressive résumé doesn't ___ well with her ignorance of some basic facts about the business.
3. By 2:00 a.m. the party was a scene of ___ frenzy.
4. She had been making outrageous statements about him to the newspapers, and he finally sued for ___ of character.
5. For kids their age they have excellent manners, and everyone admires their ___ around adults.
6. The argument had gotten fierce, but he somehow managed to ___ a remark about how they were both wrong.
7. The disappointing ___ of his career often puzzled his friends.

UNIT 6

A. Choose the closest definition:

1. malevolent   a. wishing evil b. wishing well
                  c. blowing violently d. badly done
2. malign   a. speak well of b. speak to
                  c. speak ill of d. speak of repeatedly
3. functionary   a. bureaucrat b. hard worker c. activist d. executive

4.	malicious	a. vague b. explosive c. confusing d. mean
5.	defunct	a. dead b. depressed c. defective d. deserted
6.	malnourished	a. fed frequently b. fed poorly c. fed excessively d. fed occasionally
7.	tantalize	a. visit b. satisfy c. tease d. watch
8.	dysfunctional	a. working badly b. unresponsive c. healthy d. uncaring
9.	malfunction	a. work slowly b. work improperly c. work efficiently d. work mechanically

B. Match the definition on the left to the correct word on the right:

1.	dysplasia	a.	nightmarish society
2.	dyspeptic	b.	crabby
3.	dyslexia	c.	abnormal growth
4.	dystopia	d.	reading disorder

C. Choose the word that does not belong:

1. dragon's teeth   a. dangerous b. troublesome c. sensible d. conflict

D. Fill in each blank with the correct letter:

a. dysplasia	d. tantalize	g. dystopia
b. arachnid	e. dyslexia	
c. dyspeptic	f. dragon's teeth	

1. She's been sowing ___ with her mean gossip, and by now no one in the department is speaking to anyone else.
2. The novel paints a picture of a ___ in which the effects of climate change have wrecked the social order.
3. Unlike the spiders, the ___ we call the daddy longlegs has no waist.
4. Because his ___ was discovered early, he was able to receive the special reading instruction he needed.
5. The tests had detected some suspicious cell ___, but her doctors told her not to worry since it was at a very early stage.
6. Ebenezer Scrooge, in *A Christmas Carol,* is a thoroughly ___ character.
7. He would often ___ her with talk of travelling to Brazil or India, but nothing ever came of it.

E. Indicate whether the pairs have the same or different meanings:

1.	malnourished / overfed	same ___ / different ___
2.	dyslexia / speech patterns	same ___ / different ___
3.	malign / slander	same ___ / different ___
4.	functionary / bureaucrat	same ___ / different ___
5.	malevolent / pleasant	same ___ / different ___
6.	malicious / nasty	same ___ / different ___

F. Fill in each blank with the correct letter:

a. malfunction   c. oedipal   e. dysplasia
b. functionary   d. oedipal

1. When psychologists refer to ____ behavior, they may think of a four-year-old boy competing with his father for his mother's attention.
2. In poor countries, hip ____ is rarely fixed in the early years.
3. A low-level ____ in the company handles such complaints.
4. Something that was downloaded is causing parts of the operating system to ____.
5. His fiancée looks just like his mother, and we joke with him that he's never gotten through his ____ period.

G. Complete the analogy:

1. wounded : healed :: dysfunctional : ____
   a. lame b. healthy c. crippled d. unsteady
2. reptile : snake :: arachnid : ____
   a. toad b. salamander c. bird d. scorpion
3. healthy : vigorous :: defunct : ____
   a. brainless b. failed c. strong d. unhappy
4. benevolent : wicked :: malevolent : ____
   a. evil b. silly c. noisy d. kindly
5. soldier : army :: functionary : ____
   a. anthill b. stadium c. vacation d. organization
6. jovial : merry :: dyspeptic : ____
   a. grumpy b. sleepy c. dopey d. happy
7. misbehave : scold :: malfunction : ____
   a. function b. fix c. exchange d. rearrange

UNIT 7

A. Choose the closest definition:

1. paraphrase   a. spell out b. shorten c. lengthen d. reword
2. amorous   a. friendly b. sympathetic c. loving d. kind
3. Anglophile   a. amateur fisherman b. geometry fan
   c. England-lover d. non-Hispanic
4. paramedic   a. medical technician b. hypodermic
   c. surgeon d. nurse's aide
5. amicable   a. difficult b. friendly c. curious d. lazy
6. oenophile   a. pig lover b. book lover c. word lover d. wine lover

7. paramour   a. lover b. husband c. heaven d. affection
8. enamored   a. strengthened b. engaged c. fond d. free
9. philatelist   a. stamp collector b. gem collector
                  c. wine collector d. coin collector
10. paralegal   a. lawful b. lawyer-assisting c. above the law d. barely legal
11. philanthropy a. stamp collecting b. pleasure c. dignity d. generosity
12. paramilitary a. basic-training b. skydiving c. semimilitary d. police
13. defunct   a. working b. rotten c. useless d. dreary
14. dysfunctional a. untrained b. divorced
                  c. performing poorly d. unfamiliar

B. Fill in each blank with the correct letter:

| a. paraphrase | c. paralegal | e. paramilitary |
| b. amicable | d. narcissism | f. enamored |

1. No one in her class of high-school seniors was able to ____ the proverb "Blood is thicker than water."
2. By working as a model, she could satisfy her ____ while getting paid for it.
3. Many of the crimes are apparently being carried out by members of secret ____ organizations made up of off-duty police and former soldiers.
4. At his law firm they treated almost everything involving real estate as ____ work.
5. Thoroughly ____ of the splendid Victorian house, they began to plan their move.
6. Surprisingly, her first and second husbands actually have a completely ____ relationship.

C. Complete the analogy:

1. charming : enchanting :: amorous : ____
   a. sublime b. pleasant c. likeable d. passionate
2. gentle : tender :: enamored : ____
   a. lively b. charmed c. cozy d. enraged
3. edit : revise :: paraphrase : ____
   a. dedicate b. praise c. restate d. compose
4. frozen : boiling :: amicable : ____
   a. calm b. comfortable c. shy d. unfriendly
5. friend : companion :: paramour : ____
   a. lover b. theater c. mother d. wife

D. Indicate whether the pairs have the same or different meanings:

1. philatelist / postman   same ___ / different ___
2. philanthropy / wealth   same ___ / different ___
3. oenophile / wine expert   same ___ / different ___
4. Anglophile / fish-lover   same ___ / different ___
5. philatelist / dancer   same ___ / different ___
6. secret lover / paramour   same ___ / different ___

E. Choose the correct synonym and the correct antonym:

1. venereal   a. sensual   b. intellectual   c. diseased   d. arthritic

F. Fill in each blank with the correct letter:

| a. epicure | c. Adonis | e. paramedic |
| b. narcissism | d. oenophile | f. Anglophile |

1. Filled with books about Queen Victoria, Churchill, and Henry VIII, the house was clearly home to an ____.
2. They were a very attractive couple, but their ____ often annoyed other people.
3. He's a serious ____, and you have to be brave to invite him over for dinner.
4. After a year as a ____ she knew she had the stomach for anything a doctor might have to face.
5. He's so serious about wines that it's hard to be his friend if you're not an ____.
6. Everyone thought her new boyfriend was an ____, and she liked watching girls' heads turn as they walked around campus together.

UNIT 8

A. Choose the closest definition:

1. bellicose   a. fun-loving   b. warlike   c. impatient   d. jolly
2. antebellum   a. preventive   b. unlikely   c. impossible   d. prewar
3. amicable   a. technical   b. sensitive   c. friendly   d. scenic

B. Match the definition on the left to the correct word on the right:

1. antebellum   a. quarrelsome
2. martial   b. before the war
3. rebellion   c. rebellion
4. belligerence   d. opposition to authority
5. revolt   e. related to war
6. bellicose   f. aggressiveness
7. amory   g. weapons depot

C. Indicate whether the pairs have the same or different meanings:

1. armada / fleet   same ____ / different ____
2. procrustean / merciful   same ____ / different ____
3. resurgent / revived   same ____ / different ____

4.	disarming / trucelike	same ___ / different ___
5.	vulcanize / organize	same ___ / different ___
6.	counterinsurgent / guerrilla	same ___ / different ___
7.	armory / battleship	same ___ / different ___
8.	upsurge / triumph	same ___ / different ___
9.	armistice / treaty	same ___ / different ___
10.	insurgency / inflation	same ___ / different ___

D. Fill in each blank with the correct letter:

a. bellicose	d. procrustean	g. insurgency
b. myrmidon	e. belligerence	h. disarming
c. martial	f. vulcanize	i. armistice

1. He's nothing but a ___ of the CEO, one of those creepy aides who's always following him down the hall wearing aviator sunglasses.
2. Whenever her boyfriend saw anyone looking at her, his ___ was alarming.
3. Critics condemn modern education as ___, forcing all students into narrow and limited modes of thinking.
4. Their refusal to cease work on nuclear weapons was seen as a ___ act by the neighboring countries.
5. The ___ arts of the Far East have become popular in the West as means of self-defense.
6. When Goodyear discovered how to ___ rubber, he made Henry Ford's Model T possible.
7. She had been prepared to find him terrifying, but his manner was so ___ that she relaxed almost immediately.
8. After seven long years of war, the news of the ___ was greeted with tears of joy.
9. The government had beaten back a major ___ in the 1990s, but the rebels had regrouped and new fighting had begun.

E. Fill in each blank with the correct letter:

a. antebellum	e. armada	i. upsurge
b. armistice	f. counterinsurgent	j. belligerence
c. insurgency	g. bellicose	k. disarming
d. rebellion	h. armory	l. resurgent

1. The native ___ began at midnight, when a gang of youths massacred the Newton family and set the house afire.
2. A cargo ship would suddenly be surrounded by an ___ of small pirate boats, against which it was impossible to defend itself.
3. The recent ___ in oil prices has alarmed investors, who worry that expensive oil will slow down the larger economy.
4. He's always had a ___ manner, and lots of people like him immediately because of his smile.
5. There seems to be a ___ interest in film musicals, after many years when none were being released at all.

6. Their relations during the divorce proceedings had been mostly friendly, so his ___ in the judge's chambers surprised her.
7. The ___ that was signed that year had only prevented fighting for a few months.
8. Any ___ would have to be situated well away from the battlefront, since it would be a disaster if the enemy managed to seize it.
9. The grand ___ mansion has hardly been altered since it was built in 1841.
10. The Senate Republicans, outraged by their treatment, were in a ___ mood.
11. The army was facing a large guerrilla ___ that had already taken over the fourth-largest city.
12. The rebels were becoming stronger, and the country's army and police lacked the proper training to provide an effective ___ force.

UNIT 9

A. Choose the closest definition:

1. aquaculture   a. aquarium design   b. reef diving   c. pearl fishing   d. water farming
2. aqueduct   a. channel   b. dam   c. dike   d. reservoir
3. aquanaut   a. swimmer   b. diver   c. surfer   d. pilot
4. aquifer   a. waterway   b. fishpond   c. spring   d. underground reservoir
5. urbane   a. calm   b. elegant   c. excited   d. secure
6. horticulture   a. interior decoration   b. food science   c. horse breeding   d. plant growing

B. Match the definition on the left to the correct word on the right:

1. needless repetition   a. dryad
2. flood   b. undulant
3. involving liquid   c. hydraulic
4. reflect   d. redundancy
5. tree spirit   e. inundate
6. wavelike   f. dehydrate
7. dry   g. redound

C. Complete the analogy:

1. drain : replenish :: dehydrate : ___   a. find   b. dry out   c. rehydrate   d. add
2. cattle : livestock :: fauna : ___   a. meadows   b. flowers   c. wildlife   d. trees
3. sterility : bacteria :: hydroponics : ___   a. water   b. soil   c. air   d. fire

4. canine : dog :: flora : ___
   a. oak trees b. wood nymphs c. plants d. animals
5. pneumatic : air :: hydraulic : ___
   a. solid b. gas c. liquid d. evaporation
6. evaporate : dry up :: inundate : ___
   a. flood b. drain c. wash d. irrigate
7. soak : drench :: dehydrate : ___
   a. liquidate b. dry c. dissolve d. adjust
8. nuclear : uranium :: hydroelectric : ___
   a. coal b. petroleum c. dynamics d. water
9. hobgoblin : imp :: dryad : ___
   a. moth b. oak tree c. nymph d. dragonfly

D. Choose the word that does not belong:

1. cereal   a. corn b. eggplant c. rice d. barley

E. Fill in each blank with the correct letter:

a. redound	d. aquifer	g. inundate
b. aquaculture	e. redundancy	h. aquanaut
c. undulant	f. aqueduct	

1. "Each and every" is an example of a ___ that almost everyone uses.
2. Sportsmanship and generosity always ___ to the credit of both the team and the school.
3. As an ___ she often lives underwater for several days at a time.
4. The ___ they depend on for irrigation is slowly being depleted, and the farmers are being forced to cut back on water use.
5. Wild salmon has become an expensive rarity, and ___ is the source of most of the salmon we now eat.
6. The ___ that runs through the city is an open concrete-lined river.
7. In the second movement, the composer depicts the waves of the ocean by means of lines that rise and fall in ___ patterns.
8. Piles of job applications ___ the office every day.

F. Fill in each blank with the correct letter:

a. hydroponics	c. flora	e. cereal
b. redundancy	d. redound	

1. The ___ of the West Creek Valley includes at least a dozen rare species.
2. The use of ___ and greenhouses enables the floral industry to operate year-round.
3. If our researchers receive the Nobel Prize this year, it will ___ to the university's credit for years to come.
4. The computer files contain a great deal of data ___ that isn't actually serving any purpose.
5. Corn, unknown in ancient Europe, has become a staple ___ of the modern world.

1. hydraulic / electric   same ___ / different ___
2. dehydrate / dry   same ___ / different ___
3. hydroelectric / solar-powered   same ___ / different ___
4. hydroponics / waterworks   same ___ / different ___
5. undulant / wavy   same ___ / different ___

UNIT 10

A. Complete the analogy:

1. dispute : argument :: antithesis : ___
   a. dislike b. agreement c. danger d. opposite
2. passionate : emotional :: apathetic : ___
   a. caring b. unjust c. indifferent d. dominant
3. champion : hero :: antagonist : ___
   a. comrade b. supporter c. opponent d. thug
4. humor : laughter :: pathos : ___
   a. comedy b. ridicule c. death d. pity
5. misery : joy :: antipathy : ___
   a. disgust b. confusion c. opposition d. liking
6. kindness : cruelty :: empathy : ___
   a. pity b. heartlessness c. emotion d. tears
7. cause : effect :: antigen : ___
   a. germs b. blood c. antibody d. genes
8. telephonic : electric :: telepathic : ___
   a. extrasensory b. superhuman c. airborne d. sci-fi
9. truth : fact :: antithesis : ___
   a. same b. opposite c. enemy d. friend
10. fondness : affection :: antipathy : ___
    a. love b. rejection c. solution d. distaste

B. Choose the correct synonym and the correct antonym:

1. mercurial   a. stable b. changeable c. sociable d. depressed
2. jovial   a. youthful b. mean-spirited c. merry d. magical mercurial

C. Choose the closest definition:

1. antithesis   a. opponent b. opposite c. disadvantage d. argument
2. contort   a. torture b. twist c. turn d. twirl
3. tort   a. cake b. twist c. wrong d. law

D. Fill in each blank with the correct letter:

a. idiomatic   d. telepathic   g. idiosyncrasy
b. apathetic   e. idiom   h. pathos
c. idiopathic   f. empathy

1. He had covered disasters before, but the ___ of the situation in Haiti was beyond description.
2. The public's response to studies predicting dangerous climate change was ___ for many years.
3. Almost everyone feels some ___ for a child's misery.
4. Identical twins have claimed to experience ___ communication about important events.
5. My Italian friend sometimes says "According to me" when the ___ way of saying it would be "In my opinion."
6. One famous ___ of the great pianist was playing his instrument while wearing fingerless gloves.
7. Most of us say things like "tongue in cheek" or "pound the pavement" without even knowing what an ___ is.
8. When she suspected that a patient was just imagining his symptoms, she'd tell him the illness was unusual and ___ and give him some harmless drug.

E. Choose the word that does not belong:

1. empathy a. fascination b. pity c. concern d. compassion
2. apathetic a. unfortunate b. unconcerned c. uncaring d. uninterested

F. Fill in each blank with the correct letter:

a. antigen   d. antagonist   g. mercurial
b. idiopathic   e. Junoesque
c. Triton   f. Idiom

1. Her only excuse for her behavior was her well-known ___ temper.
2. The chief ___ of the Republican Party is the Democratic Party, and vice versa.
3. When you use an ___ like "losing your edge" or "dressed to kill" in class, your foreign students are just going to be puzzled.
4. On each arm of the great candelabra was carved a ___ blowing on his conch.
5. The aging jazz singer acquired a certain ___ quality in her mature years.
6. The patient's account of her symptoms was so sketchy that for now her condition is just being called ___.
7. The initial tests look for the ___ associated with tumors of this kind.

G. Indicate whether the pairs have the same or different meanings:

1. empathy / sentimentality   same ___ / different ___
2. Junoesque / slender   same ___ / different ___
3. pathos / anger   same ___ / different ___

4.	antigen / antibody	same ___ / different ___
5.	idiosyncrasy / quirk	same ___ / different ___
6.	apathetic / indifferent	same ___ / different ___
7.	idiom / stupidity	same ___ / different ___
8.	antithesis / opposite	same ___ / different ___
9.	idiopathic / of unknown cause	same ___ / different ___
10.	antipathy / affection	same ___ / different ___
11.	idiomatic / foreign	same ___ / different ___
12.	antagonist / enemy	same ___ / different ___
13.	idiosyncrasy / oddity	same ___ / different ___
14.	jolly / jovial	same ___ / different ___

UNIT 11

A. Choose the closest definition:

1.	Pendant	a. porch b. salary c. flag d. ornament
2.	aggravate	a. lessen b. decorate c. intensify d. lighten
3.	suspend	a. study carefully b. watch closely c. slip gradually d. stop temporarily
4.	append	a. close up b. predict c. attach d. reconsider
5.	levity	a. lightness b. policy c. leverage d. literacy
6.	appendage	a. hanger b. body organ c. limb d. companion

B. Match the definition on the left to the correct word on the right:

1.	gravitate	a.	lack of seriousness
2.	levity	b.	solemn dignity
3.	aggravate	c.	serious
4.	cantilever	d.	relieve
5.	gravitas	e.	raising
6.	elevation	f.	worsen
7.	grave	g.	support beam
8.	alleviate	h.	move toward as if drawn

C. Choose the correct synonym and the correct antonym:

| 1. | olympian | a. involved b. lame c. detached d. everyday |

D. Complete the analogy:

1. cabinet : china :: Pandora's box : ___
   a. pleasures b. troubles c. taxes d. music

E. Indicate whether the pairs have the same or different meanings:

1. append / attach   same ___ / different ___
2. Promethean / creative   same ___ / different ___
3. titanic / powerful   same ___ / different ___
4. appendage / attachment   same ___ / different ___

F. Fill in each blank with the correct letter:

a. pendant   d. aggravate   g. append
b. gravitate   e. appendage   h. gravitas
c. suspend   f. grave

1. Even the smallest motion would ___ the pain in his shoulder.
2. On the organizational chart, the group appears way down in the lower left corner, looking like a minor ___ of the company.
3. At their father's funeral they showed the same solemn ___ at which they had often laughed during his lifetime.
4. This is the entire report, to which we'll ___ the complete financial data when we submit it.
5. Attracted magically by the music, all animals and natural objects would ___ toward the sound of Orpheus's lyre.
6. With the two armies moving toward the border, they knew the situation was ___.
7. Whenever his mother got wind of more bad behavior, she would ___ his allowance for a month.
8. He found himself peering at her silver ___, trying to make out the odd symbols that formed the design.

G. Match the definition on the left to the correct word on the right:

1. promotion   a.   olympian
2. stop temporarily   b.   pendant
3. dignity   c.   elevation
4. godlike   d.   gravitas
5. hanging ornament   e.   suspend

H. Fill in each blank with the correct letter:

a. alleviate   d. Promethean   g. elevation
b. titanic   e. cantilever
c. levity   f. appendage

1. In some ways, Edison's mind may have been the most ___ since Leonardo da Vinci's.
2. She hesitated to step onto the balcony, which was supported by a single ___.
3. The board meeting ended in an unusual mood of ___ when a man in a gorilla suit burst in.

4. To relieve the swelling, the doctor recommended ___ of her legs several times a day.
5. One clear and beautiful morning, a series of ___ waves swept the entire village into the sea.
6. It was a large beetle with an odd ___ coming off the top of its head.
7. The neighboring nations organized an airlift of supplies to ___ the suffering caused by the drought.

UNIT 12

A. Choose the closest definition:

1. reflective   a. merry b. thoughtful c. glowing d. gloomy
2. tutelage   a. responsibility b. protection c. instruction d. safeguard
3. hector   a. encourage b. harass c. deceive d. swear
4. intuition   a. ignorance b. quick understanding
                   c. payment d. consideration
5. deflect   a. fold over b. kneel c. turn aside d. protect
6. tutorial   a. penalty b. teacher c. classroom d. small class
7. inflection   a. style in art b. change in pitch c. muscle d. part to the rear
8. tuition   a. requirement b. instruction c. resolution d. housing
9. infraction   a. lawful act b. arrest c. piece d. violation
10. genuflect   a. kneel b. flex a muscle c. fold back
                   d. change one's tone of voice
11. fractious   a. smiling b. peaceable c. angry d. troublesome
12. Cassandra   a. optimist b. economist c. pessimist d. oculist

B. Complete the analogy:

1. clever : dull :: reflective : ___
   a. lazy b. educated. c. calm d. empty-headed
2. accent : syllable :: inflection : ___   a. note b. hint c. turn d. word
3. reflect : mirror :: deflect : ___   a. shield b. laser c. metal d. spear
4. wave : friendship :: genuflect : ___
   a. salute b. knee c. power d. obedience
5. procrustean : inflexible :: inflection : ___
   a. way of life b. tone of voice c. financial affairs d. part of speech

C. Indicate whether the pairs have the same or different meanings:

1. deflect / absorb   same ___ / different ___
2. infraction / split   same ___ / different ___

D. Match the definition on the left to the correct word on the right:

1.	tutelage	a.	instruction costs
2.	infraction	b.	quarrelsome
3.	tutorial	c.	insight
4.	fractious	d.	bending of light rays
5.	intuition	e.	guardianship
6.	fractal	f.	violation
7.	tuition	g.	individual instruction
8.	refraction	h.	self-reproducing shape

E. Fill in each blank with the correct letter:

a. intuition	d. palladium	g. refraction
b. Trojan horse	e. tutelage	
c. tuition	f. Cassandra	

1. At boarding schools, ___ isn't separated from fees for room and board.
2. A "balloon mortgage," in which the low rates for the first couple of years suddenly explode into something completely unaffordable, should be feared as a ___.
3. What he later learned about her past had confirmed his original ___ that she was not to be trusted.
4. Under the great man's ___, he slowly learned how to develop his musical ideas into full-fledged sonatas.
5. The ___ of light in a glass of water appears to bend a pencil or spoon where it enters the water.
6. The wedding rings were white gold, a mixture of gold and ___.
7. His gloomy economic forecasts earned him a reputation as a ___.

F. Choose the correct synonym and the correct antonym:

1. intuition   a. instruction   b. payment   c. logic   d. sixth sense

G. Fill in each blank with the correct letter:

a. refraction	c. fractious	e. infraction
b. hector	d. Trojan horse	f. fractal

1. Under the microscope, the bark revealed its ___ nature, reproducing its visible surface at the microscopic level.
2. The huge Senate bill was a ___, filled with items that almost none of the senators were aware of.
3. It's a ___ team, and there often seems to be no cooperation between them at all.
4. That last ___ of the rules cost their team 15 yards.
5. To rattle the other team, they usually ___ them constantly.
6. ___ of sunlight through water droplets is what produces rainbows.

UNIT 13

A. Choose the closest definition:

1. reprobate   a. prosecution b. scoundrel c. trial d. refund
2. impute   a. imply b. revise c. attribute d. defy
3. reputed   a. famous b. accused c. determined d. supposed
4. approbation   a. approval b. resolution c. reputation d. substitution
5. putative   a. assumed b. appointed c. solved d. ignored
6. disrepute   a. argument b. violence c. untruth d. disgrace
7. tutorial   a. small class b. large class c. night class d. canceled class

B. Match the definition on the left to the correct word on the right:

1. utter honesty   a. approbation
2. approval   b. reprobate
3. rascal   c. probity
4. legal process for wills   d. probate

C. Complete the analogy:

1. difficult : simple :: herculean : ____
   a. intense b. easy c. mammoth d. strong

D. Match the definition on the left to the correct word on the right:

1. impute   a. estate process
2. probate   b. very difficult
3. aegis   c. assign
4. integrity   d. probity
5. herculean   e. protection

E. Indicate whether the pairs have the same or different meanings:

1. probity / fraud   same ___ / different ___
2. syndrome / depression   same ___ / different ___
3. putative / supposed   same ___ / different ___
4. probate / trial   same ___ / different ___
5. synergy / combined action   same ___ / different ___
6. reprobate / scoundrel   same ___ / different ___
7. reputed / questioned   same ___ / different ___
8. synthesize / create from several ingredients   same ___ / different ___

F. Choose the word that does not belong:

1. Augean stable   a. purity   b. corruption   c. filth   d. herculean
2. reputed   a. known   b. reported   c. believed   d. thought

G. Indicate whether the pairs have the same or different meanings:

1. syntax / sentence structure   same ___ / different ___
2. approbation / criticism   same ___ / different ___
3. impute / compute   same ___ / different ___
4. disrepute / disgrace   same ___ / different ___
5. syndrome / group of symptoms   same ___ / different ___
6. disrepute / shame   same ___ / different ___
7. putative / natural   same ___ / different ___
8. synthesize / perform   same ___ / different ___

H. Fill in each blank with the correct letter:

     a. syntax   c. syndrome   e. synthesize
     b. aegis   d. amazon   f. synergy

1. The book manages to ____ a great deal of material that has rarely been discussed together.
2. When foreign students speak, they often employ ____ that seems odd in English but would be completely natural in their own language.
3. It wasn't obvious what kind of ____ could be achieved by merging an office-supplies company with a tractor manufacturer.
4. Doctors had become concerned about a ____ involving fever, mental confusion, and extreme weakness that had been appearing in dozens of local residents.
5. She's going on a speaking tour through the Middle East under the ____ of the State Department.
6. To everyone's surprise, he ended up marrying a robust, outdoorsy ____ an inch taller than he was.

UNIT 14

A. Choose the closest definition:

1. incoherent   a. attached   b. constant   c. controlled   d. confused
2. inherent   a. built-in   b. inherited   c. confused   d. loyal
3. adherent   a. sticker   b. stinker   c. follower   d. flower
4. iridescent   a. shimmering   b. drab   c. striped   d. watery
5. cohere   a. control   b. react   c. pause   d. unite

6. coalesce   a. begin   b. merge   c. cooperate   d. end
7. cyclopean   a. whirling   b. gigantic   c. rapid   d. circular
8. recluse   a. spider   b. hermit   c. request   d. hiding place
9. reprobate   a. researcher   b. commissioner   c. scoundrel   d. reformer

B. Complete the analogy:

1. inclusive : many :: exclusive : ____
   a. everyone   b. numerous   c. few   d. snobbish
2. monk : pray :: recluse : ____
   a. deny   b. receive   c. reclaim   d. hide
3. progress : advance :: occlusion :____
   a. dismissal   b. obstruction   c. prevention   d. denial
4. conclusion : ending :: seclusion : ____
   a. refusal   b. relaxation   c. isolation   d. denial
5. expensive : costly :: exclusive : ____
   a. indirect   b. fantastic   c. experienced   d. fashionable

C. Fill in each blank with the correct letter:

a. cohere	e. cogeneration	i. codependency
b. cohesion	f. adherent	j. syntax
c. incoherent	g. ambrosia	
d. coalesce	h. inherent	

1. Spouses of alcoholics and drug addicts meet every week in the church basement to discuss the problems of ____.
2. Paper mills are increasingly starting up ____ projects to turn their waste wood products into electricity and steam.
3. She had left Scientology and was now an ____ of the Unification Church.
4. Team ____ is always a problem early in the football season, since the kids may not know each other or understand each other's strengths and weaknesses.
5. By the time his fever reached 105°, the boy was mumbling ____ sentences.
6. Officials worry that these individual terrorist groups may be starting to ____ into one large network.
7. Mahatma Gandhi believed goodness was ____ in humans.
8. From the odd ____ of the sentences, she guessed that the writer didn't know English that well.
9. The author tries to take on so many different subjects that the book really doesn't ____ very well.
10. The dinner was nothing special, but the dessert was pure ____.

D. Indicate whether the pairs have the same or different meanings:

1.	coalesce / come together	same ____ / different ____
2.	occlusion / stroke	same ____ / different ____
3.	cogeneration / two-source power production	same ____ / different ____
4.	recluse / hermit	same ____ / different ____
5.	codependency / reliance on two parents	same ____ / different ____

6. exclusive / sole   same ___ / different ___
7. cohesion / sticking together   same ___ / different ___
8. seclusion / solitude   same ___ / different ___
9. coalesce / combine   same ___ / different ___

E. Fill in each blank with the correct letter:

a. adherent	e. cogeneration	i. occlusion
b. ambrosia	f. iridescent	j. seclusion
c. cohesion	g. codependency	
d. calypso	h. cyclopean	

1. They danced and sang to the rhythm of the ___ music long into the night.
2. The ___ of the mountain hut was just what she needed to begin serious work on her book.
3. They marveled at the massive ancient ___ walls, which truly seemed to have been built by giants.
4. The college's new ___ system will use natural gas to produce both electricity and heat.
5. The oil slick on the puddle's surface became beautifully ___ in the slanting light.
6. He's no longer really an ___ of that economic philosophy.
7. His diet had been terrible for years, so he wasn't surprised when the doctor reported a near ___ of one coronary artery.
8. Some people worry about the ___ of the European Union, especially as the number of member nations grows and national interests begin to shift.
9. He knew his daughter wasn't alcoholic, but he worried about the ___ he'd been noticing between her and her husband.
10. This sauce tastes like ___!

UNIT 15

A. Choose the closest definition:

1. terminus   a. heat source b. endpoint c. final exam d. period
2. subsequent   a. unimportant b. early c. first d. later
3. interminable   a. remarkable b. unthinkable c. reliable d. eternal
4. zephyr   a. stormy blast b. icy rain c. light shower d. gentle breeze
5. terminal   a. fatal b. technical c. verbal d. similar
6. sequential   a. important b. noticeable c. in order d. distant
7. indeterminate   a. lengthy b. uncertain c. unending d. likely
8. confine   a. erect b. restrict c. ignore d. lock out

9. non sequitur   a. distrust b. refusal c. odd statement d. denial
10. finite   a. vast b. finished c. nearby d. limited
11. incoherent   a. clear b. uncertain c. confused d. unknown
12. inherent   a. local b. inherited c. acquired d. built-in

B. Fill in each blank with the correct letter:

a. confine	e. finite	i. sequential
b. consequential	f. subsequent	j. indeterminate
c. definitive	g. infinitesimal	
d. non sequitur	h. interminable	

1. The detectives insisted on a detailed and ___ account of the evening's events.
2. An ___ speck of dust on the lens can keep a CD player from functioning.
3. He's hopeless at conversation, since practically everything he says is a ___.
4. The lab results were ___, and he was told to wait a week before having another blood test.
5. He sometimes thought that missing that plane had been the most ___ event of his life.
6. Let's ___ this discussion to just the first part of the proposal.
7. We have a ___ number of choices, in fact maybe only three or four.
8. This may be the best book on the subject so far, but I wouldn't call it ___.
9. There were a few arguments that first day, but all the ___ meetings went smoothly.
10. I had an ___ wait in the doctor's office and didn't get home until 6:00.

C. Fill in each blank with the correct letter:

a. terminus	d. cynosure	g. terminal
b. halcyon	e. indeterminate	h. zephyr
c. interminable	f. aeolian harp	

1. In those ___ summers, he and his cousins spent every day sailing and swimming in the blue Wisconsin lakes.
2. On fair days a gentle ___ would blow from morning until night.
3. New Yorkers tend to think of their city as the ___ of the nation.
4. Their land extends all the way out to the ___ of the little peninsula.
5. He was a man of ___ age, and mysterious in other ways as well.
6. Every so often, a breeze would spring up and the ___ in the window would emit its beautiful harmonies.
7. He gave ___ lectures, and I usually dozed off in the middle.
8. Last week we assumed his condition was ___; today no one is making predictions.

D. Choose the correct synonym and the correct antonym:

1. terminal   a. first b. final c. highest d. deathlike

E. Indicate whether the pairs have the same or different meanings:

1. cynosure / guide   same ___ / different ___
2. halcyon / delightful   same ___ / different ___
3. definitive / clear-cut   same ___ / different ___

F. Match the definition on the left to the correct word on the right:

1. non sequitur   a. limit
2. confine   b. limited
3. definitive   c. ultimate
4. subsequent   d. tiny
5. finite   e. out-of-place statement
6. sequential   f. following
7. infinitesimal   g. significant
8. consequential   h. ordered

UNIT 16

A. Choose the odd word:

1. protracted   a. lengthened b. continued c. circular d. extended
2. traction   a. grip b. drive c. pulling force d. steering
3. retract   a. unsay b. withdraw c. force d. take back
4. intractable   a. unbelievable b. uncontrollable c. stubborn d. difficult

B. Match the definition on the left to the correct word on the right:

1. go backward   a. retract
2. repeat   b. traction
3. lengthy   c. Scylla and Charybdis
4. difficult   d. regress
5. unsay   e. reconcile
6. draw out   f. intractable
7. refresh   g. reiterate
8. equal perils   h. protract
9. bring into agreement i. protracted
10. pulling force   j. rejuvenate

C. Fill in each blank with the correct letter:

a. remorse	d. reiterate	g. reconcile
b. rebut	e. reciprocal	h. rejuvenate
c. revoke	f. regress	i. nemesis

1. State officials may ___ the factory's permit to release larger amounts of heated water into the river.
2. Her outburst at her daughter left her filled with ___ for days afterward.
3. These spas always promise to ___ your skin, and often your spirit as well.
4. She's trying to ___ the image she had of her friend with what she's recently learned about him.
5. The governor has been trying to ___ these new charges against him for days without success.
6. In eighth grade his ___ was a disagreeable girl named Rita who liked playing horrible little tricks.
7. Sometimes our 15-year-old just seems to ___ and start acting the way he did when he was two years younger.
8. In almost every speech she tries to ___ the same few points, since she doesn't trust the voters to remember them otherwise.
9. An American university may have a ___ arrangement with a European university, whereby each agrees to take the other's students for a year.

D. Choose the correct synonym and the correct antonym:

1. nemesis   a. ally   b. no one   c. enemy   d. bacteria

E. Fill in each blank with the correct letter:

a. rebut	e. revoke	i. chimera
b. reciprocal	f. gorgon	j. intractable
c. nemesis	g. traction	k. reconcile
d. retract	h. remorse	

1. Her boss was a ___ who terrorized the office.
2. The truck was getting almost no ___ on the snowy road.
3. The prison situation is ___, and likely to get worse.
4. He tried to ___ his statement the next day, but the damage had been done.
5. She was sure her old ___ was plotting to get her fired.
6. ___ over the accident seems to be the main cause of his depression.
7. They haven't been able to ___ the results of the two studies, which came to very different conclusions.
8. When she tried to ___ the claims her opponent had made, the crowd broke out in jeers.
9. Because of numerous violations, the city is threatening to ___ the nightclub's license to operate.
10. Expensive golf courses sometimes have ___ agreements that enable members to use courses in other cities for the same price.
11. As he aged he began to think the CIA was watching him, and even though it was just a ___ it caused him a lot of anxiety.

F. Complete the analogy:

1. wrath : anger :: Scylla and Charybdis : ___
   a. rage   b. double peril   c. ferocity   d. whirlpools

G. Indicate whether the pairs have the same or different meanings:

1. revoke / cancel   same ___ / different ___
2. rebut / send back   same ___ / different ___
3. regress / backslide   same ___ / different ___
4. reiterate / modernize   same ___ / different ___
5. remorse / regret   same ___ / different ___
6. rejuvenate / return   same ___ / different ___
7. reconcile / fight back   same ___ / different ___
8. reciprocal / mutual   same ___ / different ___
9. rejuvenate / renew   same ___ / different ___
10. reiterate / restate   same ___ / different ___
11. rebut / disprove   same ___ / different ___

UNIT 17

A. Indicate whether the pairs have the same or different meanings:

1. mediate / exchange   same ___ / different ___
2. Paleozoic / of the period about 10,000 years ago   same ___ / different ___
3. intermediary / agent   same ___ / different ___
4. paleography / study of ancient writings   same ___ / different ___
5. mediocrity / ordinariness   same ___ / different ___
6. Paleolithic / Old Stone Age   same ___ / different ___
7. median / so-so   same ___ / different ___
8. paleontology / study of past geological periods   same ___ / different ___
9. Holocene / recent era   same ___ / different ___

B. Fill in each blank with the correct letter:

a. mediocrity	e. hologram	i. mediate
b. holistic	f. intermediary	j. holocaust
c. paleontology	g. Holocene	
d. median	h. Paleolithic	

1. After going on a fossil dig in Africa in junior year, he decided to pursue graduate work in ___.
2. He likes wearing a T-shirt with a large ___ on the chest and watching people's reactions to the way it changes as they walk by.
3. The school's wrestling team includes a couple of big guys, but the ___ weight is only about 160 pounds.
4. His doctor favors a ___ approach to achieving wellness, but she'll prescribe standard drugs for serious illnesses.

5. The creation of the United Nations was intended to, among other things, prevent another ____ from ever occurring.
6. There are still a few hunting-and-gathering tribes on earth who live the way all of humankind lived at the beginning of the ____.
7. The two kids are always fighting, and their father's main job is to ____ their disputes.
8. These illegal arms deals usually require an ____ who knows both languages and is trusted by both parties.
9. She'd been expecting a lot from the kids in the advanced-placement class, so she was dismayed by the ____ of the first papers they passed in.
10. We found some chipped-stone arrowheads and took them to a local professor, who identified them as products of the ____ period.

C. Choose the closest definition:

1. holistic   a. wholesome b. herbal c. complete d. whole-oriented
2. potential   a. regulation b. influence c. impact d. possibility

D. Fill in each blank with the correct letter:

a. Paleolithic	e. inanimate	i. Pyrrhic victory
b. magnanimous	f. paleography	j. Midas touch
c. Paleozoic	g. Croesus	
d. Sisyphean	h. paleontology	

1. My grandfather has never had any money, but his brother is rich as ____.
2. With his specialty in ____, he spent much of his time on the rivers of Peru looking for rocks with ancient carvings.
3. We all know it's ridiculous to curse at ____ objects when it's just our own clumsiness that's at fault.
4. The triumphant corporate takeover proved to be a ____, since the resulting debt crippled the corporation for years.
5. In his victory speech he was ____ to his opponents, promising them an important role in his government.
6. The wall paintings date from the end of the ____, just before the beginning of settled farming villages.
7. Millions of kids are fascinated by dinosaurs, but not many will go on to study ____ in college.
8. Insects, reptiles, amphibians, and primitive fish inhabited the earth during the ____ era, but not mammals.
9. Her wealthy father had always had the ____, and his money-making genius was still a mystery to her.
10. For a mother of nine, laundry and ironing can seem ____ in their endlessness and drudgery.

E. Choose the word that does not belong:

1. Sisyphean   a. difficult b. unending c. demanding d. rolling
2. Croesus   a. rich b. powerful c. impoverished d. successful
3. Midas touch   a. talented b. unsuccessful c. rich d. prosperous

4. Pyrrhic victory   a. unqualified   b. costly   c. dangerous   d. destructive

F. Match the definition on the left to the correct word on the right:

1.	holocaust	b.	3-d image
2.	holistic	c.	current human era
3.	Holocene	d.	mass destruction
4.	hologram	e.	concerned with the whole

UNIT 18

A. Choose the closest definition:

1.	surmount	a. increase b. overcome c. look through d. reject
2.	surfeit	a. surplus b. waves c. conclusion d. topic
3.	surreal	a. excessive b. artistic c. secret d. dreamlike
4.	subversion	a. sabotage b. undertow c. turnover d. overture

B. Indicate whether the pairs have the same or different meanings:

1.	superfluous / enormous	same ___ / different ___
2.	insuperable / impossible	same ___ / different ___
3.	supersede / replace	same ___ / different ___
4.	superlative / outstanding	same ___ / different ___
5.	insuperable / excellent	same ___ / different ___

C. Fill in each blank with the correct letter:

a. kudos	e. superfluous	i. surcharge
b. subliminal	f. subjugate	j. anaerobic
c. acme	g. subconscious	k. referendum
d. subversion	h. supersede	

1. Stealing elections through fraud represents a ___ of democracy.
2. The advice my doctors have been giving me about my condition has been ___, since I've known all these facts for years.
3. Accident-prone people may have a ___ desire to do themselves harm.
4. Napoleon hoped to ___ all of Europe and make it his empire.
5. To help balance its budget, the city is now considering adding a ___ to all speeding tickets.
6. At the ___ of his racing career, Bold Ruler won the Kentucky Derby.
7. He claims the ice cubes in whiskey ads contain images that send ___ messages to readers.

8. The committee voted to submit the new zoning plan to the voters in a special ____.
9. A young Korean pianist has been winning ____ from critics worldwide.
10. She does a lot of ____ muscle training, but just running for the bus will leave her panting.
11. The new version of the software will naturally ____ any previous versions, even if some users think it's not an improvement.

D. Fill in each blank with the correct letter:

a. surfeit	e. supersede	i. eureka
b. superlative	f. trauma	j. surreal
c. surcharge	g. insuperable	k. subjugate
d. superfluous	h. surmount	l. subconscious

1. Again and again she had overcome what seemed to be ____ odds.
2. It took her just a few weeks to recover from the physical ____, but the emotional scars were still with her years later.
3. The governor is calling for a ____ on all packaged snack foods with low nutritional value.
4. In Iraq, many years of government brutality failed to fully ____ the people called the Kurds.
5. There was something ____ about gazing out from the deck of a luxurious cruise ship at the primitive huts lining the islands' shores.
6. ____! I knew I'd find that file sooner or later!
7. This new set of regulations will ____ the ones we've been working under for the last five years.
8. The movie had received ____ reviews, and we were looking forward to seeing it.
9. Was it some ____ fear that made her forget the interview?
10. Even though we know hardly any facts about the divorce, there's already been a ____ of talk on the radio about it.
11. When he was wheeled out to accept the award, most of the audience realized for the first time what terrible difficulties he had had to ____.
12. A lot of the language in these student essays is ____, since it just repeats things that have already been said in different words.

E. Complete the analogy:

1. alas : disappointment :: eureka : ____
   a. distress b. woe c. distance d. discovery
2. drama : play :: trauma : ____
   a. wound b. harm c. mind d. emotion
3. unconscious : aware :: subliminal : ____
   a. underneath b. noticeable c. deep d. regular
4. criticism : error :: kudos : ____
   a. praise b. prestige c. blame d. achievement

F. Match the definition on the left to the correct word on the right:

1.	surcharge	a.	rise above
2.	subjugate	b.	secret effort to overthrow
3.	surfeit	c.	excess
4.	subconscious	d.	not strong enough to be sensed
5.	surmount	e.	dreamlike
6.	subversion	f.	extra fee
7.	surreal	g.	conquer
8.	subliminal	h.	beneath the level of consciousness

UNIT 19

A. Choose the closest definition:

1. excrescence   a. disgust b. outgrowth c. extremity d. garbage
2. hedonism   a. preference for males b. habit of gift-giving
   c. tendency to conceal feelings d. love of pleasure
3. degrade   a. praise b. outclass c. lose d. lower
4. accretion   a. agreement b. eruption c. decision d. buildup
5. retrograde   a. failing b. forward c. sideways d. backward
6. increment   a. entrance b. slight increase c. construction d. income
7. gradation   a. program in a series b. stage in a series
   c. eventual decline d. definite improvement
8. crescent   a. semicircle b. pastry c. sickle shape d. buildup
9. gradient   a. graph b. slope c. road d. steps
10. stoic   a. pleasure-seeking b. bullying c. repressed d. unaffected by pain

B. Fill in each blank with the correct letter:

a. agnostic	d. degrade	g. gradient
b. gradation	e. retrograde	h. prognosis
c. cognitive	f. incognito	

1. Psychology is not entirely a ____ science, since it deals with behavior as well as the mind.
2. Each subtle ____ of color seemed more beautiful as the sun slowly set.
3. Movie stars often go out in public ____, in faded sweatshirts, worn-out pants, and sunglasses.
4. The trail's ____ for the first part of the race was gentle, but after three miles it became quite steep.
5. She has strong opinions about lots of public issues, but she's an ____ about foreign policy.

6. The ___ for the world's climate in the next century is uncertain.
7. Once a thriving democracy, the country lapsed into dictatorship in the 1970s, a ___ step that it's still recovering from.
8. By all means apologize for your mistake, but don't ___ yourself.

C. Choose the closest definition:

1. degrade
   a. reduce in size b. raise in esteem c. lower in rank d. increase in importance
2. hedonism
   a. fear of heights b. hatred of crowds c. liking for children d. love of pleasure
3. gradation
   a. step in a series b. show in a series c. novel in a series d. speech in a series
4. retrograde
   a. moving in reverse b. grading again c. primitive d. switching grades

D. Match the definition on the left to the correct word on the right:

1. question-and-answer   a.   accretion
2. accumulation   b.   platonic
3. nonsexual   c.   Socratic

E. Fill in each blank with the correct letter:

a. crescent	d. prognosis	g. Socratic
b. gradient	e. stoic	
c. platonic	f. cognitive	

1. He bore all his financial losses with the same ___ calm.
2. They're worried about their son's mental health, though the doctors say his ___ skills are fine.
3. The ___ method is inappropriate for normal courtroom interrogation.
4. The hammer and sickle on the Soviet Union's flag oddly resembled the Islamic star and ___.
5. The doctor's ___ is guarded, but she is cautiously optimistic that recovery will be complete.
6. The dinner was good, but saying that it approached the ___ ideal of a meal was probably too much.
7. In Japan, the track for a mountain cable car climbs at a ___ of an astonishing 31 degrees.

F. Complete the analogy:

1. portion : segment :: increment : ___
   a. inroad b. inflation c. increase d. instinct
2. cavity : hole :: excrescence : ___
   a. growth b. deposit c. residue d. toad

G. Choose the correct *antonym*:

1. incognito   a. indoors b. in disguise c. as oneself d. as you were

H. Indicate whether the pairs have the same or different meanings:

1. agnostic / complex   same ___ / different ___
2. crescent / pinnacle   same ___ / different ___
3. cognitive / digestive   same ___ / different ___
4. excrescence / ugliness   same ___ / different ___
5. incognito / hospitable   same ___ / different ___
6. increment / excess   same ___ / different ___
7. prognosis / outlook   same ___ / different ___
8. accretion / destruction same ___ / different ___

UNIT 20

A. Choose the closest definition:

1. abjure   a. take up b. damn c. reject d. include
2. factotum   a. manufacturer b. untruth c. dilemma d. assistant
3. ad hoc   a. for this purpose b. permanent
                c. long-range d. for many reasons
4. perjury   a. cleansing b. lying under oath c. theft d. court decision
5. ex post facto a. in anticipation b. sooner or later
                c. coming after d. someday
6. facilitate   a. guide b. build c. order d. obstruct
7. de jure   a. by a judge b. by a lawyer c. by law d. by a jury
8. ad hominem   a. based on personalities b. based on logic
                c. based on issues d. based on sexual preference
9. jurisprudence a. legal philosophy b. legal agreement
                c. senior judge d. cautious ruling
10. facile   a. tough b. quiet c. familiar d. easy
11. de facto   a. in transit b. in effect c. in debt d. in theory

B. Fill in each blank with the correct letter:

a. factotum   d. de jure   g. perjury
b. jurisprudence   e. facilitate   h. abjure
c. facile   f. factor

1. She was probably committing ___ when she swore that she had spent the
   night alone at home.

2. As soon as the party agrees to ____ violence, we're ready to allow them to participate in elections.
3. She was quick-witted, but her reasoning was often ____ and not deeply thoughtful.
4. As the company's ____, she often felt overworked and underappreciated.
5. The support of the financial industry would greatly ____ the passage of the bill.
6. The ____ power of the prime minister was considerable, but all real power was held by the army.
7. The main ____ in their decision to build was their desire for a completely "green" home.
8. Although her own philosophy of ____ is liberal, most observers think her interpretations of the law as a judge have been balanced.

C. Match the definition on the left to the correct word on the right:

1. nothingness   a.   annulment
2. undo   b.   nullify
3. cancellation   c.   nullity
4. invalid   d.   null

D. Complete the analogy:

1. past : previous :: ex post facto : ____
   a. beforehand b. afterward c. during d. actually
2. personal : impersonal :: ad hominem : ____
   a. to the time b. to the issue c. to the end d. to the maximum

E. Fill in each blank with the correct letter:

| a. null | c. facilitate | e. nullity |
| b. nullify | d. annulment | f. a. ad hoc |

1. An ____ committee was named to come up with ideas for redecorating the waiting room.
2. If the judge's decision goes against the government, it will ____ a 10-year-old state law.
3. Her lawyer is going to argue that the first trial was a ____ because some of the jurors missed whole days of testimony.
4. They finally realized they would need a real-estate agent to ____ the sale of the property.
5. After five years and no children, she asked the church for an ____ of the marriage.
6. We're claiming the contract is ____ and void because the other company failed to do what it had agreed to.

F. Indicate whether the pairs have the same or different meanings:

1. de facto / actually   same ____ / different ____
2. annulment / undoing   same ____ / different ____

3.   facilitate / ease   same ___ / different ___
4.   de jure / based on law   same ___ / different ___
5.   factor / element   same ___ / different ___
6.   jurisprudence / legal beliefs   same ___ / different ___
7.   factotum / expert   same ___ / different ___
8.   perjury / testimony   same ___ / different ___
9.   facile / practical   same ___ / different ___
10. abjure / reject   same ___ / different ___
11. facile / handy   same ___ / different ___
12. null / not in effect   same ___ / different ___

UNIT 21

A. Choose the closest definition:

1.   beneficiary   a. benefit b. prayer c. recipient d. contributor
2.   discordant   a. insulting b. relieved c. unlimited d. conflicting
3.   opus   a. achievement b. composition c. burden d. talent
4.   benediction   a. blessing b. gift c. saint d. favor
5.   cordial   a. hateful b. friendly c. fiendish d. cool
6.   gratuity   a. fee b. service c. obligation d. tip
7.   benefactor   a. supporter b. priest c. donation d. kindness
8.   concord   a. generosity b. straightness c. agreement d. pleasure
9.   gratis   a. irritating b. grateful c. inexpensive d. free
10. benevolence   a. value b. kindness c. luck d. approval
11. accord   a. harmonize b. accept c. distress d. convince
12. gratify   a. unify b. donate c. satisfy d. modify
13. gratuitous   a. pleasant b. unnecessary c. happy d. satisfying
14. benediction   a. slogan b. prayer c. greeting d. expression
15. discordant   a. energetic b. temporary c. phony d. clashing

B. Choose the correct antonym:

1.   accord   a. harmonize b. strengthen c. differ d. agree
2.   cordial   a. lazy b. cool c. terrific d. heartfelt
3.   concord   a. belief b. conflict c. deception d. peace

C. Indicate whether the pairs have the same or different meanings:

1.   gratify / gladden   same ___ / different ___
2.   gratuity / tip   same ___ / different ___
3.   ingratiate / contribute same ___ / different ___
4.   gratuitous / deserved   same ___ / different ___

D. Match the definition on the left to the correct word on the right:

1.	giver	a.	accord	
2.	gift receiver	b.	concord	
3.	heartfelt	c.	benefactor	
4.	goodwill	d.	discordant	
5.	disagreeing	e.	beneficiary	
6.	grant	f.	cordial	

E. Fill in each blank with the correct letter:

a. ingratiate   d. benevolence   g. onus
b. magnum opus   e. discordant
c. gratis   f. opus

1. His latest ____ is a set of songs on poetry by Pablo Neruda.
2. The souvenirs were distributed ____ to anyone who stopped to see the display.
3. Her attempts to ____ herself with the new management were resented by the other workers.
4. Now that they have apologized, the ____ is on you to do the same.
5. Each side's anger at the other has set a sadly ____ tone for the negotiations.
6. The Rite of Spring is often regarded as Igor Stravinsky's ____.
7. He wouldn't even have a place to live if it weren't for the ____ of his wealthy godfather.

F. Complete the analogy:

1. gladden : delight :: gratify : ____   a. please   b. depress   c. amaze   d. surprise
2. greeting : farewell :: benediction : ____
   a. motto   b. speech   c. curse   d. saying
3. favor : prefer :: gratify : ____   a. use   b. please   c. thank   d. repay
4. bonus : salary :: gratuity : ____
   a. obligation   b. thankfulness   c. refusal   d. bill
5. entertain : joke :: ingratiate : ____   a. flatter   b. devour   c. vibrate   d. criticize
6. praise : compliment :: onus : ____
   a. load   b. habit   c. obligation   d. reputation
7. lender : borrower :: benefactor : ____
   a. giver   b. beneficiary   c. participant   d. partner
8. liking : appreciation :: benevolence : ____
   a. opinion   b. sentimentality   c. interest   d. generosity
9. necessary : needed :: gratuitous : ____
   a. thankless   b. unthinking   c. welcome   d. uncalled-for
10. patient : doctor :: beneficiary : ____
    a. tycoon   b. investor   c. lover   d. benefactor

UNIT 22

A. Choose the closest definition:

1. endemic   a. common b. absent c. infectious d. occasional
2. populous   a. well-liked b. foreign c. numerous d. obscure
3. demotic   a. devilish b. common c. cultural d. useful
4. populace   a. politics b. numerous c. masses d. popularity
5. congregation a. anthill b. gathering c. hearing d. church
6. demagogue   a. medium-sized city b. fiery politician
                c. democratic socialist d. new democracy
7. populist   a. communist b. campaigner c. socialist
                d. believer in the people
8. demographic a. describing politics b. describing populations
                c. describing policies d. describing epidemics
9. vox populi   a. public policy b. public survey
                c. public opinion d. public outrage
10. aggregate   a. nuisance b. assembly c. pile d. sum total

B. Complete the analogy:

1. obedient : tame :: egregious : ____
   a. crowded b. uncrowded c. blatant d. fair
2. series : sequence :: aggregate : ____
   a. individual b. collection c. attack d. annoyance
3. tear : mend :: segregate : ____
   a. mix b. sort c. send away d. refine
4. location : place :: congregation : ____
   a. birds b. whales c. group d. temple
5. obnoxious : pleasant :: egregious : ____
   a. boring b. bothersome c. unpleasant d. unnoticeable

C. Fill in each blank with the correct letter:

a. congregation	d. populist	g. populace
b. demographic	e. detritus	h. egregious
c. segregate	f. aggregate	

1. The child had tried to hide his mistake with an ____ lie.
2. The general ____ has never cared much about foreign policy except when the country goes to war.
3. ____ surveys often divide the U.S. population by income and education.
4. Battlefield medics were forced to ____ the hopeless cases from the other casualties.
5. Taken in the ____, these statistics are very disturbing.
6. The steep bank had become a dumping ground, and ____ of all kinds lay at the bottom.
7. The ____ grew silent as the first strains of the wedding march sounded.

8. She ran her campaigns as a ____, a champion of the common man, though she herself had a great deal of money.

D. Indicate whether the pairs have the same or different meanings:

1. demotic / common   same ___ / different ___
2. populist / politician   same ___ / different ___
3. endemic / locally common   same ___ / different ___
4. populace / popularity   same ___ / different ___
5. demographic / phonetic   same ___ / different ___
6. vox populi / mass sentiment   same ___ / different ___
7. demagogue / prophet   same ___ / different ___
8. populous / well-loved   same ___ / different ___
9. vox populi / public opinion   same ___ / different ___
10. open courtyard / atrium   same ___ / different ___

E. Fill in each blank with the correct letter:

a. segregate   c. hoi polloi   e. delegation
b. cornucopia   d. atrium   f. detritus

1. We sent a two-person ____ off to the restaurant to choose supper for everyone.
2. The storm waves had left the beach littered with ____.
3. When the economy is good, a job fair can be a ____ of employment opportunities.
4. The new office building was designed around a wide, sunlit ____ with a fountain and small trees.
5. She says she and her fellow stars would never go near a restaurant where the ____ might be eating.
6. Let's ____ the bad fruit from the rest to prevent the rot from spreading.

UNIT 23

A. Choose the closest definition:

1. servile   a. efficient b. pleasant c. humble d. unnerving
2. pact   a. bundle b. form c. agreement d. presentation
3. implacable   a. impossible to place b. impossible to change
                  c. impossible to say d. impossible to like
4. subservient   a. arrogant b. submissive c. demanding d. underneath
5. placebo   a. one-celled animal b. medical instrument
                  c. harmless substance d. peaceful mood

6. endemic   a. local b. neighborly c. sensational d. foreign
7. populous   a. numerous b. populated c. popular d. common
8. demotic   a. reduced b. common c. upper-class d. demented

B. Match the definition on the left to the correct word on the right:

1.	*pace*	a.	solemn agreement
2.	placidity	b.	unyielding
3.	pact	c.	contrary to the opinion of
4.	placebo	d.	soothe
5.	charisma	e.	to make peaceful
6.	pacify	f.	harmless substitute
7.	placate	g.	one who opposes war
8.	pacifist	h.	peacefulness
9.	implacable	i.	personal magnetism

C. Fill in each blank with the correct letter:

a. placebo	d. pace	g. placidity
b. pacifist	e. implacable	h. pacify
c. placate	f. pact	i. dogma

1. It took a week of bringing flowers home every day to ____ his wife.
2. An ____ mob had been demonstrating outside the presidential palace for two weeks now, with their numbers growing from day to day.
3. Treating epilepsy and depression by stimulating the muscles with electrical current was medical ____ for years, but today no one is doing it anymore.
4. ____ some of the younger scholars, no good evidence has been found that Japan was involved in the incident.
5. The cease-fire ____ that had been reached with such effort was shattered by the news of the slaughter.
6. The group of patients who were given a ____ did as well as those who were given the real drug.
7. The world watched in amazement as the gentle ____ Gandhi won India its independence with almost no bloodshed.
8. Her soft lullabies could always ____ the unhappy infant.
9. The ____ of the quiet countryside was soothing after a week in the city.

D. Complete the analogy:

1. fashionable : stylish :: serviceable : ____
   a. useless b. devoted c. fundamental d. adequate
2. turmoil : conflict :: placidity : ____
   a. peace b. dullness c. trouble d. smoothness
3. freedom : liberty :: servitude : ____
   a. determination b. arrangement c. slavery d. work
4. considerate : thoughtless :: subservient : ____
   a. boastful b. bossy c. decisive d. unique

5. monarchy : king :: oligarchy : ___
a. dictator b. ruling group c. emperor d. totalitarian
6. dominant : aggressive :: servile : ___
a. saving b. sensitive c. obedient d. forgetful
7. capable : helpless :: serviceable : ___
a. useless b. useful c. practical d. formal

E. Indicate whether the pairs have the same or different meanings:

1. subservient / military   same ___ / different ___
2. serviceable / usable   same ___ / different ___
3. ostracize / shun   same ___ / different ___
4. servitude / enslavement   same ___ / different ___
5. servile / humble   same ___ / different ___
6. peace lover / pacifist   same ___ / different ___

F. Fill in each blank with the correct letter:

a. charisma   d. ostracize   g. servitude
b. placate   e. dogma   h. pacify
c. pace   f. oligarchy

1. Unable to calm the growing crowd, he finally ordered the police to ___ the area by force.
2. The country has a president, of course, but everyone knows he's just the front man for a shadowy ___.
3. Her theory was hotly debated, since it disagreed with the established ___.
4. The children at the orphanage lived in a condition of genuine ___, often working from dawn to dusk.
5. Though he hasn't been convicted of anything yet, it's obvious that the community is going to ___ him.
6. Attracting and motivating such a terrific faculty required a principal of great personal ___.
7. Her boss had flown into a rage that morning, and it had taken her two hours to ___ him.
8. ___ my many critics, I have never had reason to change my views on the subject.

UNIT 24

A. Match the definition on the left to the correct word on the right:

1.	nomenclature	a.	wrong name
2.	misnomer	b.	mistake
3.	nominal	c.	rule by men
4.	ignominious	d.	unreliability
5.	fallacious	e.	wrong
6.	fallacy	f.	naming system
7.	infallible	g.	in name only
8.	fallibility	h.	perfect

B. Complete the analogy:

1. repulsive : attractive :: ignominious : ___
   a. favorite b. honorable c. horrible d. disgraceful
2. tag : label :: pseudonym : ___
   a. last name b. title c. maiden name d. alias

C. Fill in each blank with the correct letter:

a. fallacious	e. infallible	i. nomenclature
b. antonym	f. eponymous	j. misnomer
c. fallibility	g. fallacy	
d. patronymic	h. pseudonym	

1. The Restaurant Alain Savoy is the ___ establishment belonging to the great French chef.
2. At first glance the article's claims sounded interesting, but it wasn't hard to discover the basic ___ they were based on.
3. The best ___ for "popular" is "unpopular," not "shy."
4. The ___ of these tests has been shown again and again, but some doctors keep using them.
5. In a Russian family in which the father is named Fyodor, a boy's ___ would be Fyodorovich and a girl's would be Fyodorevna.
6. He was born Vlad Butsky, but he writes under the ___ Vance Bond.
7. Each time a new insect is discovered, strict rules of ___ help determine what its name will be.
8. Saying that one cool summer disproves the whole idea of global warming is obviously ___ and no one really believes it.
9. "Panama hat" is a ___, since the hats have actually always been made in Ecuador.
10. In his teens he had read book after book about gambling strategies, all of which were claimed by their authors to be ___.

D. Choose the closest definition:

1. zealot   a. spokesman b. leader c. joker d. fanatic

2. nominal   a. trifling   b. important   c. by name   d. serious
3. pseudonym   a. alias   b. phony   c. made-up word   d. honorary title
4. patronymic   a. client's name   b. name based on your father's
         c. last name   d. first name
5. antonym   a. technical name   b. word with related meaning
         c. word with opposite meaning   d. third name
6. eponymous   a. having several rulers   b. written by three people
         c. borrowed from literature   d. taken from a name

E. Choose the correct synonym and the correct antonym:

1. delphic   a. clear   b. dark   c. stormy   d. ambiguous

F. Fill in each blank with the correct letter:

a. sibyl	d. nominal	g. patronymic
b. misnomer	e. exodus	h. nomenclature
c. zealot	f. ignominious	

1. It's a community pool, and the fee we pay each time we use it is only ___.
2. Her departure from the company led to an ___ of other employees.
3. "Friend" is a ___ for Charlotte; "rival" is more like it.
4. Stevenson was originally a ___ ("Steven's son"), which was later sometimes shortened to Stevens.
5. The first public attempts to test the antiballistic missiles ended in ___ failure.
6. She won her reputation as the office ___ after her third successful prediction of who would get married next.
7. The person who discovers a previously unknown plant usually gets to name it, but the ___ must follow a strict set of rules.
8. Meeting him again after five years, she was dismayed to discover that he'd become a religious ___ who could talk about no other subject.

UNIT 25

A. Choose the closest definition:

1. peripheral   a. supplementary   b. around a tooth
                   c. wandering   d. dangerous
2. periodontal   a. visual   b. inside a tooth   c. around a tooth   d. wandering
3. peripatetic   a. wandering   b. unemployed
                   c. surrounding   d. old-fashioned
4. perimeter   a. factor   b. characteristic   c. supplement   d. boundary

5. alter ego   a. church structure   b. bad conscience
                  c. intimate friend   d. self-love
6. egocentric   a. group-centered   b. centered on the mind
                  c. self-centered   d. mentally ill.

B. Indicate whether the pairs have the same or different meanings:

1. epiphyte / parasite   same ___ / different ___
2. epitaph / grave inscription   same ___ / different ___
3. ethnocentric / group-centered   same ___ / different ___

C. Fill in each blank with the correct letter:

a. epicenter	e. epithet	i. id
b. epiphyte	f. egocentric	j. libido
c. ethnocentric	g. epilogue	k. alter ego
d. epitaph	h. eccentric	

1. The doctor warned her that her ___ would be reduced while she was on the medication.
2. She is such a close friend that she seems like my ___.
3. The earth's orbit around the sun is ___ rather than perfectly circular.
4. Is any ___ inscribed on Grant's Tomb?
5. Andrew Jackson's ___, describing his lean toughness, was "Old Hickory."
6. There's nothing wrong with liking yourself so long as you don't become ___.
7. Her visit in the spring was a kind of ___ to our relationship, which had really ended two months earlier.
8. Luckily, the quake's ___ was far away from any human settlement.
9. The ___ is completely primitive and reacts unthinkingly according to the pleasure-pain principle.
10. She claims that his remarks show an ___ bias against foreign cultures.
11. An ___ seems to live on air and water alone.

D. Complete the analogy:

1. prologue : beginning :: epilogue : ___   a. start   b. end   c. book   d. drama
2. mob : crowd :: ego : ___   a. self   b. other   c. friend   d. same

E. Match the definition on the left to the correct word on the right:

1.	epicenter	a.	central point
2.	epiphyte	b.	centered on one's own group
3.	egocentric	c.	grave inscription
4.	epitaph	d.	self-centered
5.	ethnocentric	e.	non-parasitic plant growing on another
6.	epithet	f.	descriptive nickname
7.	eccentric	g.	placed off-center
8.	epilogue	h.	surrounding

F. Choose the correct synonym and the correct antonym:

1. peripheral   a. central b. logical c. sincere d. secondary
2. perimeter   a. essence b. edge c. center d. spurt
3. peripatetic   a. stay-at-home b. exact c. wandering d. imprecise

G. Fill in each blank with the correct letter:

a. epicenter   e. perimeter   i. periodontal
b. peripheral   f. ego   j. libido
c. id   g. peripatetic
d. epithet   h. eccentric

1. Those who enter the monastery don't lose their ____, just their opportunity to satisfy it.
2. His habit of wearing purple socks and white sneakers to the office was considered harmlessly ____.
3. He has such a massive ____ that no praise seems to satisfy him.
4. Because of deer, she needed to put up a fence along the ____ of the garden.
5. The wildest of these underground comic books seem to be a pure expression of the teenage ____.
6. In his youth he had been amazingly ____, hitchhiking thousands of miles on three continents.
7. She works hard at being outrageous, and it's not the first time she's been at the ____ of a controversy.
8. Regular flossing can prevent most ____ disease.
9. "Gray-eyed" is the standard ____ used to describe the goddess Athena.
10. ____ vision is part of what most eye doctors test in their patients.

UNIT 26

A. Choose the closest definition:

1. cross-cultural   a. intensively cultivated b. between two or more cultures
   c. combining fruits and vegetables d. combining art and music
2. urbanization   a. moving to cities b. street construction
   c. becoming citylike d. mass transit
3. horticulture   a. intellectual knowledge b. science of growing plants
   c. animal science d. horse breeding
4. acculturation   a. developing cultural institutions
   b. turning woods into farmland
   c. acquiring aspects of another culture
   d. appreciation of music and dance

5. interurban   a. densely populated   b. between cities
                          c. from the inner city   d. within the city
6. spartan   a. cheap   b. Greek   c. severe   d. luxurious
7. subculture   a. group within a culture   b. cultivation below ground
                          c. goth kids   d. small garden
8. peripheral   a. auxiliary   b. central   c. relating to the sun   d. philosophical
9. periodontal   a. relating to feet   b. around the sun
                          c. around the teeth   d. around a corner
10. urbane   a. foolish   b. old-fashioned   c. dependable   d. sophisticated
11. sybaritic   a. pleasure-seeking   b. free of luxury   c. sisterly   d. ice-cold
12. exurban   a. high-rise   b. crowded   c. above the city   d. beyond the suburbs

B. Fill in each blank with the correct letter:

a. exurban	e. interurban	i. laconic
b. urbane	f. urbanization	j. politicize
c. acculturation	g. horticulture	k. solecism
d. cross-cultural	h. subculture	

1. Like most farmers, he's fairly ____, but when he says something it's usually worth listening to.
2. ____ had proceeded swiftly over the previous ten years, and shopping malls had replaced the cozy streets of the old suburb.
3. He can't go to a cocktail party without committing at least one ____ and offending a couple of people.
4. Their next-door neighbors were an ____ couple who threw lively parties where you could meet writers, artists, designers, and media people.
5. His wife's background in ____ led them to plant a large fruit orchard and build a huge greenhouse for flower cultivation.
6. The Congress has managed to ____ an issue that always used to be thought of as a private matter.
7. In his teens he became part of a Web-based ____ whose members were devoted to raising poisonous reptiles.
8. ____ railways have begun making a comeback as city dwellers have become increasingly concerned about climate change.
9. In their ____ home, 25 miles from the city, they looked out on a small field and woods.
10. A ____ study had revealed far greater levels of anxiety in middle-class Americans than in middle-class Scandinavians.
11. After the island was acquired by Japan around 1910, the population began undergoing rapid ____, eventually giving up its native language.

C. Match the definition on the left to the correct word on the right:

1.	politicize	a.	huge urban area
2.	megalopolis	b.	shrewdly sensitive
3.	solecism	c.	high part of a city
4.	acropolis	d.	turn into a political issue
5.	politic	e.	goof

D. Fill in each blank with the correct letter:

a. solecism	d. megalopolis	g. laconic
b. politic	e. cross-cultural	h. politicize
c. sybaritic	f. acropolis	

1. Chicago itself has fewer than 3 million inhabitants, but the ____ that includes Milwaukee and Madison has over 14 million.
2. The mood at the resort was ____, and the drinking and dancing continued long into the night.
3. He knew it was never ____ to mention his own children's achievements around his brother, whose oldest son was in prison.
4. He was interested in ____ studies that showed that these kinds of cancers don't appear in African tribal populations.
5. The city government buildings occupied an ____, high above the factories that lined the riverbank.
6. Her father-in-law was ____ in her presence but extremely talkative around his son.
7. Most voters thought it was unfortunate that the candidates had actually managed to ____ a traffic accident.
8. After encountering the fifth ____ in the report, we began to lose faith in the writer.

UNIT 27

A. Choose the closest definition:

1. tort   a. deformity b. law c. product d. wrongful act
2. contort   a. perform b. twist c. squeeze d. expand
3. capitulate   a. nod b. yield c. resist d. fall in
4. extort   a. obtain by force b. pay up c. engage in crime d. exterminate
5. tortuous   a. painful b. winding c. harmful d. monstrous
6. stigma   a. sting b. statue c. stain d. stalk
7. capitalism   a. free-enterprise system b. common-property state
         c. socialist democracy d. controlled economy

B. Match the definition on the left to the correct word on the right:

1. recapitulate   a. free-market system
2. decapitate   b. behead
3. capitalism   c. surrender
4. capitulate   d. summarize

C. Choose the correct synonym and the correct antonym:

1. corpulent   a. slim   b. spiritual   c. overweight   d. bodily
2. corporal   a. military   b. bodily   c. nonphysical   d. reasonable

D. Fill in each blank with the correct letter:

a. incorporate	f. tortuous	k. decapitate
b. capitalism	g. corporeal	l. contort
c. tort	h. recapitulate	m. apologia
d. corporal	i. extort	
e. capitulate	j. corpulent	

1. She's too proud to ___ to her rivals on this point without getting something major in return.
2. The flogging of sailors was once a common form of ___ punishment in the British navy.
3. ___ is the economic system in most of the world's countries today, but in many of these the government also plays a large role.
4. At 300 pounds, President Taft was often referred to as ___, especially by his enemies.
5. The guillotine was used in France to ___ criminals before capital punishment was outlawed there.
6. We carefully made our way down the steep and ___ trail.
7. All the sports channels constantly ___ the highlights of recent games.
8. He tried to ___ a B from his math teacher by saying that, if he couldn't play because of bad grades, they'd lose and everyone would blame her.
9. We hope to ___ suggestions from everyone on the board into our final proposal.
10. The footprints on the rug suggested that their mysterious nighttime visitor had been something more ___ than a ghost.
11. She was able to ___ her body so as to fit entirely into a box 20 inches square.
12. In a ___ case, unlike a criminal case, the government doesn't get involved.
13. His book is an ___ for his entire life, which may cause his enemies to rethink their opinion of him.

E. Complete the analogy:

1. demanding : effortless :: tortuous : ___
   a. twisting   b. winding   c. straight   d. descending

F. Indicate whether the pairs have the same or different meanings:

1. corporeal / substantial   same ___ / different ___
2. corpus delicti / basic evidence   same ___ / different ___
3. corpulent / boring   same ___ / different ___
4. incorporate / leave out   same ___ / different ___
5. corporal / military   same ___ / different ___

G. Fill in each blank with the correct letter:

a. decapitate	e. corpus delicti	i. recapitulate
b. extort	f. tortuous	j. incorporate
c. corporeal	g. stigma	
d. habeas corpus	h. apologia	

1. When she woke from her coma, she reported the experience of floating in the air and looking down on her ____ body.
2. She began a long and ____ explanation of why she had stayed out so late, but her parents weren't buying it.
3. Our professor is always careful to ____ her main points at the end of each class.
4. In the 1950s the ____ of divorce was strong enough that a divorced man almost couldn't run for high office.
5. She was forced to practically ____ the money from her husband with threats.
6. All of the elements were available to establish the ____ of the defendant's crime.
7. In this report she hoped to ____ all the research she'd been doing for the last year.
8. In legal systems without ____, individuals are often locked up for years without ever knowing the charges against them.
9. In their harsh justice system, the standard practice was to lop off the hands of minor offenders and ____ serious criminals.
10. At a scientific conference in July she delivered a convincing ____ for the unusual methods that had drawn so much criticism.

UNIT 28

A. Choose the closest definition:

1. codify — a. conceal b. list c. disobey d. interpret
2. instrumental — a. instructive b. intelligent c. helpful d. fortunate
3. codicil — a. small fish b. one-tenth
   c. amendment to a will d. legal objection
4. cicerone — a. guide b. cartoon character c. orator d. lawyer
5. deconstruction — a. analysis b. destruction c. breaking d. theory
6. codex — a. private seal b. handwritten book
   c. secret letter d. coded message
7. draconian — a. clever b. massive c. disastrous d. severe
8. decode — a. explain b. conceal c. symbolize d. disguise

B. Match the definition on the left to the correct word on the right:

1.	codicil	a.	interpret
2.	codex	b.	old type of book
3.	decode	c.	will addition
4.	codify	d.	organize laws

C. Complete the analogy:

1. rule : regulation :: stricture : ____
   a. criticism b. injury c. dislike d. bravery
2. solve : figure out :: construe : ____
   a. build b. misspell c. tighten d. interpret
3. description : portrayal :: deconstruction : ____
   a. demolition b. interpretation c. transference d. translation
4. inspect : examine :: construe : ____
   a. condemn b. continue c. contend d. interpret
5. consumer goods : cars :: infrastructure : ____
   a. foundation b. surface c. bridges d. boats
6. practical : effective :: instrumental : ____
   a. hardworking b. tool-shaped c. instructional d. useful

D. Indicate whether the pairs have the same or different meanings:

1. infrastructure / dome   same ___ / different ___
2. constrict / assemble   same ___ / different ___
3. deconstruction / demolition   same ___ / different ___
4. restrictive / limiting   same ___ / different ___
5. instrumental / melodic   same ___ / different ___
6. construe / explain   same ___ / different ___
7. vasoconstrictor / Amazon snake same ___ / different ___
8. thespian / teacher   same ___ / different ___
9. stricture / tightening   same ___ / different ___
10. classify / codify   same ___ / different ___
11. codicil / addition   same ___ / different ___

E. Choose the correct synonym and the correct antonym:

1. decode   a. translate b. recover c. encode d. transmit

F. Fill in each blank with the correct letter:

a. stricture	e. restrictive	i. stringent
b. codicil	f. thespian	j. codex
c. philippic	g. draconian	k. constrict
d. vasoconstrictor	h. infrastructure	

1. The collapsing bridge was only the latest evidence of the city's deteriorating ____.

2. In everyone there is a bit of the ____ yearning for a stage.

3. A ___ to the environmental treaty provided for a special exception for three African countries.
4. Historians point to the ___ treaty terms of World War I as a major cause of World War II.
5. Soon after the banking scandal hit the newspapers, a new set of ___ regulations was announced.
6. She was given a ___ for the tooth extraction, but there was some bleeding anyway.
7. These deposits are beginning to ___ the coronary arteries to a dangerous degree.
9. In the rare-book room of the library, he found another ___ containing three long poems in Old English.
10. There were several ___ clauses in the house contract, including one that required weekly mowing of the lawn.
11. His most famous speech was a ___ on the Vietnam War delivered on the floor of the Senate in 1967.

UNIT 29

A. Choose the closest definition:

1.	mortality	a. deadliness b. danger c. disease d. death rate
2.	posterior	a. on the front b. on the back c. underneath d. on top
3.	amortize	a. bring back b. pay down c. make love d. die off
4.	postmodern	a. ultramodern b. traditional c. contemporary d. mixing styles
5.	mortify	a. weaken b. bury c. embarrass d. kill
6.	moribund	a. deathlike b. unhealthy c. lethal d. dying
7.	retribution	a. gift b. revenge c. response d. duplication
8.	posthumous	a. before the event b. born prematurely c. occurring after death d. early in development
9.	postmortem	a. after the event b. before the event c. caused by the event d. causing the event

B. Indicate whether the pairs have the same or different meanings:

1.	attribute / donate	same ___ / different ___
2.	posterior / front	same ___ / different ___
3.	tributary / small lake	same ___ / different ___
4.	a priori / determined later	same ___ / different ___
5.	tribute / praise	same ___ / different ___
6.	mortify / stiffen	same ___ / different ___

7. retribution / revenge same ___ / different ___
8. amortize / pay down same ___ / different ___
9. tribute / praise same ___ / different ___
10. dying / moribund same ___ / different ___

C. Fill in each blank with the correct letter:

a. a priori	d. constrict	g. mortify
b. amortize	e. moribund	h. a posteriori
c. rigor mortis	f. memento mori	i. mortality

1. By the 1960s, most of the textile industry had moved south, and the mill town seemed ___.
2. Most people don't spend much time thinking about their ___ until they're in their thirties or forties.
3. The philosopher published his own ___ proof of the existence of God.
4. They should be able to ___ their mortgage completely by the time they retire.
5. To judge from the degree of ___, she appeared to have died no later than 4:00 a.m.
6. Some religious sects still engage in acts designed to ___ the flesh.
7. She feared that marriage and a family would ___ her life unbearably.
8. This art critic takes the ___ position that if Pablo Picasso painted it, it's a masterpiece of modern art.
9. Just accept those first gray hairs as a little ___.

D. Complete the analogy:

1. postscript : letter :: postmortem : ___
   a. examination b. death c. body d. morgue
2. prenatal : before birth :: posthumous : ___
   a. after birth b. before life c. after death d. famous
3. exterior : interior :: posterior : ___
   a. frontal b. behind c. beside d. above
4. hip-hop : music :: postmodern : ___
   a. tradition b. design c. style d. architecture

E. Fill in each blank with the correct letter:

a. tributary	d. mortality	g. rigor mortis
b. a posteriori	e. attribute	h. tribute
c. retribution	f. moribund	i. memento mori

1. The ___ rates from these kinds of cancer have been going down as new treatments have been adopted.
2. The insult had left her seething, and within minutes she had begun planning her terrible ___.
3. As ___ to his huge achievements, the university announced that it would be naming the new science building for him.

4. It was a major ___ to the Amazon, but until 1960 no one but the native Indians had ever attempted to reach its source.
5. That yappy little dog makes the ___ assumption that he's what keeps me from breaking into the house.
6. The death was so recent that ___ hadn't yet set in.
7. The preserved body sits on a chair behind glass in public view like a strange ___.
8. He wants to ___ his success entirely to his own brains and energy, forgetting that not everyone is born with $30 million to play with.
9. The newspaper has suffered declines in both advertisements and readership over the last few years and is clearly ___.

UNIT 30

A. Choose the closest definition:

1. quid pro quo   a. proven truth   b. philosophical question
                     c. mystery   d. something given in return
2. sine qua non   a. requirement   b. exception   c. allowance   d. objection
3. propriety   a. misbehavior   b. suitability   c. harassment   d. drama

B. Match the definition on the left to the correct word on the right:

1.	formal	a.	prophylaxis
2.	introduction	b.	protrude
3.	backer	c.	prologue
4.	disease prevention	d.	pro bono
5.	forward-looking	e.	promulgate
6.	unpaid	f.	proponent
7.	declare publicly	g.	pro forma
8.	jut out	h.	proactive

C. Indicate whether the pairs have the same or different meanings:

1. proprietary / public   same ___ / different ___
2. quid pro quo / synonym   same ___ / different ___
3. appropriate / take   same ___ / different ___
4. prologue / extension   same ___ / different ___
5. expropriate / seize   same ___ / different ___
6. proactive / anticipating   same ___ / different ___
7. propriety / ownership   same ___ / different ___
8. prophylaxis / support   same ___ / different ___
9. promulgate / broadcast   same ___ / different ___

10. protrude / bulge   same ___ / different ___

D. Fill in each blank with the correct letter:

a. pro bono	d. promulgate	g. proactive
b. proponent	e. pro forma	h. protrude
c. prophylaxis	f. prologue	i. in memoriam

1. For the doctor, ___ requires the use of gloves and sometimes masks, and constant hand washing throughout the day.
2. The only part of being a lawyer that she really liked was her ___ work helping poor families with their housing problems.
3. Talk-show hosts were helping to ___ a made-up story about a scandal involving the First Lady.
4. At the end of each year, the magazine includes a section called "___," which lists all the important figures who died that year.
5. Economists worry that these scattered bank failures may turn out to be a ___ to a serious financial crisis.
6. He's gotten terribly thin, and the bones of his arms now ___ from under his skin.
7. Her apology was strictly ___, and didn't sound sincere at all.
8. The company has never spent much time thinking about its future, and it really needs to become more ___.
9. He claims we're falling behind in education, which is why he's a ___ of a longer school year.

E. Complete the analogy:

1. grant : award :: expropriate : ___   a. find b. want c. move d. claim
2. accept : receive :: appropriate : ___   a. send b. lose c. take d. offer
3. night : dark :: sine qua non : ___
    a. necessary b. nonessential c. thorough d. objective
4. monetary : money :: proprietary : ___
    a. prosperity b. property c. profit d. protection
5. reprimand : scolding :: encomium : ___
    a. warm drink b. warm thanks c. warm toast d. warm praise
6. habit : practice :: propriety : ___
    a. appropriateness b. property c. behavior d. proportion
7. appropriate : take :: expropriate : ___
    a. proclaim b. seize c. expel d. complete

F. Fill in each blank with the correct letter:

a. pro forma	d. proponent	g. appropriate
b. encomium	e. in memoriam	h. pro bono
c. sine qua non	f. quid pro quo	i. propriety

1. The company's new standards of ___ prohibited taking any large gifts from salespeople.

2. He has always been a ____ of women's issues, particularly government-funded day care.
3. The monument listed the brave men and women who had died in the war, under the words "____."
4. Most of the ____ work he's done has been for environmental groups that can't afford legal fees.
5. The application process was just ____, since they had already promised her the job.
6. The Congressman's vote was seen as a ____ for the insurance industry's campaign contributions.
7. She claimed there was no such thing as the ____ of a successful novel, since great novels are so different.
8. Most of her speech was devoted to a glowing ____ to her staff members.
9. The legislature had decided to ____ funds for new harbor facilities.

UNIT 31

A. Choose the closest definition:

1. convoluted — a. spinning b. babbling c. grinding d. winding
2. turbine — a. whirlpool b. engine c. headdress d. carousel
3. fortitude — a. armor b. endurance c. skill d. weapon
4. evolution — a. process of development b. process of democracy c. process of election d. process of elimination
5. perturb — a. reset b. inset c. preset d. upset
6. forte — a. discipline b. force c. castle d. special strength
7. voluble — a. whirling b. unpleasant c. talkative d. garbled
8. turbulent — a. churning b. turning c. yearning d. burning
9. fortification — a. diet b. exercise c. stronghold d. belief
10. devolve — a. hand down b. hand in c. turn up d. turn around
11. turbid — a. flat b. calm c. confused d. slow
12. fortify — a. attack b. strengthen c. struggle d. excite
13. per se — a. if not b. of course c. free of charge d. as such

B. Indicate whether the pairs have the same or different meanings:

1. turbine / plow — same ____ / different ____
2. carpe diem / look ahead — same ____ / different ____
3. evolution / extinction — same ____ / different ____
4. turbid / muddy — same ____ / different ____

C. Match the definition on the left to the correct word on the right:

1.	voluble	a.	murky
2.	turbine	b.	chatty
3.	evolution	c.	seething
4.	turbid	d.	complicated
5.	devolve	e.	turning engine
6.	perturb	f.	degenerate
7.	convoluted	g.	disturb
8.	turbulent	h.	progress

D. Fill in each blank with the correct letter:

a. turbine	e. carpe diem	i. devolve
b. fortification	f. forte	j. fortitude
c. per se	g. a fortiori	
d. fortify	h. caveat emptor	

1. She had hired a highly experienced deputy, hoping to ___ many of her responsibilities onto him.
2. Carpentry isn't his ___, but he could probably build something simple like a bed.
3. They could ___ their theory by positive results from some more experiments.
4. The article isn't really about surgery ___, but it talks about several issues that are closely related to it.
5. The last Spanish ___ along the river proved to be the most difficult one for the French forces to take.
6. Whenever she was on the verge of despair, she remembered her grandfather's words about ___ being the character trait most important for success.
7. If Britain can't afford a space program, then ___ neither can a much poorer country like India.
8. When you go out to buy a used car, the best advice, warranty or no warranty, is still "___."
9. The roar of the ___ was so loud they couldn't hear each other.
10. Their motto is "___," and the two of them have more fun than anyone I know.

E. Complete the analogy:

1. warranty : guarantee :: caveat emptor : ___
   a. explanation b. warning c. endorsement d. contract

F. Choose the correct *antonym*.

1.	forte	a. weak point b. sword c. quarrel d. pinnacle
2.	fortify	a. construct b. reinforce c. supply d. weaken

G. Choose the closest definition:

1. voluble   a. argumentative   b. mumbly   c. speechless   d. talkative
2. turbulent   a. unending   b. swirling   c. muddy   d. angry
3. perturb   a. soothe   b. restore   c. park   d. upset
4. devolve   a. decay   b. turn into   c. suggest   d. improve
5. convoluted   a. disorderly   b. complex   c. discouraged   d. superior

UNIT 32

A. Choose the closest definition:

1. aerate   a. fly   b. inflate   c. supply with oxygen   d. glide
2. tabula rasa   a. partial truth   b. complete ignorance
                    c. slight contamination   d. pure trash
3. terra incognita   a. new information   b. unknown cause
                    c. unexplored territory   d. old suspicion

B. Match the definition on the left to the correct word on the right:

1. theater area   a. mariner
2. blue-green gem   b. terrestrial
3. under the ground   c. marina
4. earthly   d. terrarium
5. near the sea   e. maritime
6. contained habitat   f. nautical
7. seaman   g. subterranean
8. maritime   h. aquamarine
9. small harbor   i. parterre

C. Complete the analogy:

1. crepe : pancake :: parterre : ____
   a. balcony   b. planet   c. garden   d. parachute
2. motel : motorist :: marina : ____   a. dock   b. pier   c. sailor   d. boat
3. aquarium : water :: terrarium : ____   a. plants   b. turtles   c. rocks   d. earth
4. urban : city :: maritime : ____   a. beach   b. dock   c. sea   d. harbor
5. barrier : stop :: impetus : ____   a. force   b. drive   c. trip   d. work
6. aquatic : water :: terrestrial : ____   a. sea   b. land   c. forest   d. mountain
7. pink : red :: aquamarine : ____   a. blue   b. watery   c. turquoise   d. yellow
8. logger : lumberjack :: mariner : ____   a. doctor   b. lawyer   c. chief   d. sailor
9. submarine : underwater :: subterranean : ____
   a. blue   b. belowground   c. hollow   d. rumbling

D. Choose the word that does not belong:

1. mariner   a. sailor   b. seaman   c. crew member   d. archer
2. maritime   a. coastal   b. nautical   c. oceangoing   d. lakeside

E. Fill in each blank with the correct letter:

a. anaerobic   d. terra incognita   g. aerobic
b. referendum   e. aerial   h. impetus
c. aerate   f. tabula rasa

1. The entire field of quantum physics is ___ to me.
2. ___ photos of the earthquake's destruction showed dramatically how it had cut straight through the city.
3. The planning board submitted its proposal to the voters as a nonbinding ___.
4. As for knowledge about home repair, his mind is a ___.
5. She goes running four times a week, and on the other days she does ___ workouts at the gym.
6. The ___ for this latest big research effort is a prize that's being offered by a foundation.
7. The only ___ exercise he gets is biking, but he goes so slowly that it hardly even counts.
8. Since oxygen improves the taste of most red wines, wine lovers will usually ___ a newly opened bottle for a few minutes before drinking.

F. Indicate whether the pairs have the same or different meanings:

1. aerial / lively   same ___ / different ___
2. aquamarine / navy blue   same ___ / different ___
3. subterranean / underground   same ___ / different ___
4. aerate / supply with air   same ___ / different ___
5. mariner / sailor   same ___ / different ___
6. terrestrial / earthly   same ___ / different ___
7. aerobic / involving oxygen   same ___ / different ___
8. marina / dock   same ___ / different ___
9. aerial / performed in the air   same ___ / different ___
10. terrarium / garden   same ___ / different ___
11. anaerobic / inflated   same ___ / different ___
12. parterre / fancy garden   same ___ / different ___

UNIT 33

A. Choose the closest definition:

1. acerbic   a. spicy   b. tangy   c. mild   d. stinging
2. revivify   a. revive   b. reclaim   c. retain   d. restrain
3. vivacious   a. sweet-tempered   b. loud   c. lively   d. gluttonous
4. modus vivendi   a. pie with ice cream   b. compromise
       c. stalemate   d. immoral conduct
5. acme   a. monument   b. peak   c. honor   d. award
6. vivisection   a. living area   b. animal experimentation
       c. experimental treatment   d. removal of organs
7. modus operandi   a. procedure   b. way of moving   c. crime   d. arrest
8. acrid   a. pleasant   b. crazed   c. irritating   d. soothing
9. precursor   a. shadow   b. forerunner   c. follower   d. oath
10. acrimony   a. breakup   b. dispute   c. bitterness   d. custody
11. bon vivant   a. dieter   b. partyer   c. chocolate candy   d. nightclub act

B. Fill in each blank with the correct letter:

a. concurrent	e. cursory	i. primer
b. exacerbate	f. convivial	j. curriculum vitae
c. precursor	g. discursive	
d. vivacious	h. opprobrium	

1. The warm days in March were a ___ to spring floods that were sure to come.
2. They often joined their neighbors for a ___ evening of Scrabble or charades.
3. After only a ___ look at the new car, he knew he had to have it.
4. She came to enjoy the ___ style of the older, rambling essays.
5. She sent out a ___ full of impressive educational and professional credentials.
6. ___ has been heaped on the school board from angry parents on both sides of the issue.
7. Convention-goers had to decide which of the ___ meetings to attend.
8. She had written a little ___ on volunteering, which she was now expanding into a full-length book.
9. Dr. Moss warned him that any drinking would only ___ his condition.
10. She had been a ___ teenager, but had become rather quiet and serious by her thirties.

C. Indicate whether the pairs have the same or different meanings:

1. acrimony / divorce payment   same ___ / different ___
2. concurrent / simultaneous   same ___ / different ___
3. acrid / dry   same ___ / different ___
4. modus operandi / way of life   same ___ / different ___

5. acerbic / harsh   same ___ / different ___
6. cursory / hurried   same ___ / different ___
7. exacerbate / worsen   same ___ / different ___

D. Complete the analogy:

1. cursory : brief :: carnal : ___
   a. musical b. festive c. deadly d. sexual
2. funny : comical :: acerbic : ___
   a. distrustful b. sarcastic c. witty d. cheerful
3. experiment : subject :: vivisection : ___
   a. botany b. biology c. bacteria d. animals

E. Match the definition on the left to the correct word on the right:

1.	forerunner	a.	cursory
2.	hasty	b.	precursor
3.	rambling	c.	concurrent
4.	simultaneous	d.	discursive

F. Fill in each blank with the correct letter:

a. revivify	e. opprobrium	i. vivacious
b. modus operandi	f. acrimony	j. modus vivendi
c. acrid	g. bon vivant	k. acerbic
d. vivisection	h. exacerbate	l. curriculum vitae

1. The list of new demands only served to ___ the crisis.
2. Her short stories are her main qualification for the job, but the college needs her ___ as well.
3. As the daughter of a ___, she was used to having her parents leave her with a babysitter most evenings while they enjoyed themselves in the downtown bars and restaurants.
4. With four or five ___ comments she managed to annoy or insult almost everyone in the room.
5. A group of new young teachers had managed to ___ the school.
6. The independent-minded teenager and her overprotective parents struggled to arrive at a ___ that both sides could accept.
7. Marie is the ___ one and Jan is the serious one.
8. Even for a child-custody case, the ___ between the parties was unusual.
9. The ___ fumes in the plant irritated his eyes and nose for several days.
10. The usual ___ for the songwriters was for one to write the lyrics first and then for the other to compose the music.
11. He was horrified by ___, and even protested the dissecting of frogs in biology class.
12. When a neo-Nazi group marched down Pennsylvania Avenue, it was greeted with loud ___ from egg-throwing anti-Nazi demonstrators.

UNIT 34

A. Choose the closest definition:

1. effusive   a. emotional b. gradual c. continual d. general
2. purgative   a. secret agent b. bleaching agent
   c. road agent d. cleansing agent
3. suffuse   a. overwhelm b. flow c. spread through d. inject
4. catharsis   a. explosion b. cleansing c. pollution d. cough
5. transfusion   a. revision b. change c. transfer d. adjustment
6. purgatory   a. near heaven b. place of punishment
   c. evacuation d. place of earthly delights
7. profusion   a. distinction b. abundance c. addition d. completion
8. revivify   a. retreat b. rewrite c. reappear d. refresh

B. Indicate whether the pairs have the same or different meanings:

1. resolution / attitude   same ___ / different ___
2. suffuse / fill   same ___ / different ___
3. soluble / explainable   same ___ / different ___
4. profusion / amount   same ___ / different ___
5. absolution / forgiveness   same ___ / different ___
6. effusive / gushy   same ___ / different ___
7. dissolution / disintegration   same ___ / different ___
8. transfusion / improvement   same ___ / different ___

C. Fill in each blank with the correct letter:

a. purgative	c. ethos	e. thesis
b. expurgate	d. purge	f. purgatory

1. For a sick person, waiting for medical test results can feel like ___.
2. She wrote her ___ on the portrayal of women in the works of Nathaniel Hawthorne.
3. When taken in moderate quantities, the ___ effects of bran can be healthful.
4. Concerned that the workers might be forming a union, the president considered trying to ___ the entire department.
5. Filmmakers must sometimes ___ entire scenes from their films to receive an acceptable rating
6. There's something very wrong with a company's ___ when the employees who get ahead are the ones who tell on their friends.

D. Match the definition on the left to the correct word on the right:

1. place of misery
2. remove offensive material
3. spread over
4. purifying
5. excessive pride
6. remove impure elements
7. soluble
8. dissolution

b. hubris
c. purge
d. breakup
e. purgative
f. suffuse
g. expurgate
h. dissolvable
i. purgatory

E. Complete the analogy:

1. freezing : melting :: dissolution : ____
   a. unification b. separation c. death d. defiance
2. repair : fix :: purge : ____
   a. purify b. smooth c. weaken d. support
3. request : plea :: absolution : ____
   a. accusation b. forgiveness c. requirement d. loss
4. erase : delete :: expurgate : ____
   a. confess b. read c. censor d. scrub
5. determined : hesitant :: soluble : ____
   a. moist b. dry c. unexplainable d. possible
6. generous : stingy :: effusive : ____
   a. emotional b. thoughtful c. restrained d. passionate
7. puzzle : mystery :: resolution : ____
   a. determination b. delay c. detection d. demand
8. disease : cure :: dissolution : ____
   a. disintegration b. unification c. departure d. solidity

F. Fill in each blank with the correct letter:

a. absolution	d. catharsis	g. thesis
b. profusion	e. resolution	h. hubris
c. purge	f. transfusion	i. ethos

1. It seems like ____ to brag about a victory before it has been won.
2. Three new young staff members were hired this year, and they've given the whole place a real ____ of energy.
3. He'd been very nervous about seeing her again, so when she smiled at him it felt like a kind of ____.
4. She hates school, and she lacks the ____ to complete her high-school equivalency degree on her own.
5. He had to revise his ____ twice before being granted his master's degree.
6. The outburst seemed to ____ the crowd of its anger.
7. His painting is obviously a kind of ____ for him, and his works are filled with violent images.
8. She joined the church because of its ____ of tolerance and social service.
9. The bower was hung with roses blooming in great ____.

A. 1.a 2.d 3.c 4.b 5.c 6.b 7.b 8.d   B. 1.d 2.a 3.a 4.d 5.a 6.a 7.a 8.d
C. 1.f 2.e 3.a 4.d 5.b 6.c   D. 1.b 2.f 3.e 4.d 5.a 6.ab 7.g 8.c
E. 1.a 2.a 3.b 4.c 5.c 6.c 7.a 8.b   F. 1.b 2.f 3.a 4.e 5.g 6.c 7.d 8.a 9.b

UNIT 35

A. Choose the closest definition:

1. dislodge   a. drink slowly b. scatter c. make pale d. remove
2. diffident   a. angry b. different c. aggressive d. shy
3. discredit   a. cancel a bank card b. show to be untrue
                    c. dissolve d. lower one's grade
4. credence   a. creation b. belief c. doubt d. destruction
5. dissuade   a. remove b. break up c. advise against d. sweep away
6. credible   a. believable b. acceptable c. praiseworthy d. remarkable
7. disorient   a. confuse b. disagree c. take away ` hide

B. Complete the analogy:

1. genuflect : kneel :: affidavit : ___   a. financial affairs
   b. courtroom testimony c. legal advice d. sworn statement
2. truce : treaty :: ultimatum : ___
   a. decision b. negotiation c. threat d. attack
3. credence : trust :: discursive : ___
   a. fast b. slow-moving c. wide-ranging d. all-knowing
4. fake : fraudulent :: bona fide : ___
   a. copied b. certain c. authentic d. desirable
5. support : assist :: dissuade : ___
   a. distrust b. convince c. soothe d. discourage

C. Match the definition on the left to the correct word on the right:

1. bad faith   a. perfidy
2. emotional disorder   b. credible
3. acceptance   c. diffident
4. perplex   d. credulity
5. sworn document   e. credo
6. damage a reputation   f. affidavit
7. principles   g. fiduciary
8. believable   h. credence
9. trust-based   i. resurgent
10. pry loose   j. disorient
11. trustfulness   k. dissuade
12. revived   l. discredit
13. convince otherwise   m. dislodge
14. timid   n. neurosis

D. Indicate whether the pairs have the same or different meanings:

1. insurgency / uprising   same ___ / different ___
2. credulity / distrust   same ___ / different ___
3. upsurge / increase   same ___ / different ___
4. dislodge / deflate   same ___ / different ___
5. armada / fleet   same ___ / different ___
6. perfidy / disloyalty   same ___ / different ___
7. discredit / mislead   same ___ / different ___

E. Fill in each blank with the correct letter:

a. perfidy	f. credo	k. credence
b. colossus	g. dissuade	l. ultimatum
c. credible	h. affidavit	m. neurosis
d. diffident	i. fiduciary	
e. credulity	j. bona fide	

1. She gave little ___ to his story about his deranged girlfriend and the kitchen knife.
2. Their account of the burglary didn't strike investigators as ___, and the insurance company refused to pay.
3. For many years Microsoft has remained the ___ of the software industry, feared by all its competitors.
4. The family trust had been so badly mismanaged that it appeared there had been a violation of ___ responsibility.
5. The company's odd but charming ___ was "Don't be evil."
6. When peace negotiations fell apart, an angry ___ was issued by the government.
7. Her ___ is enormous; no story in the supermarket tabloids is too far-fetched for her.
8. To ensure that all reservations are ___, the cruise line requires a nonrefundable deposit.
9. His particular ___ was a fear of heights.
10. She's the only person who could possibly ___ him from proceeding with this foolish plan.
11. He's so ___ that you'd never believe he gives talks in front of international organizations.
12. The ___ stated that no oral agreement had ever been made.
13. For her own best friend to take up with her former husband was ___ that could never be forgiven.

UNIT 36

A. Choose the closest definition:

1. crypt   a. code   b. granite   c. tomb   d. church
2. deduction   a. addition   b. flirtation   c. total   d. reasoning
3. cryptography   a. gravestone writing   b. physics writing
                   c. code writing   d. mathematical writing
4. mea culpa   a. through my eyes   b. through my fault
                   c. through my door   d. through my work

B. Indicate whether the pairs have the same or different meanings:

1. cryptic / gravelike   same ___ / different ___
2. meander / wind   same ___ / different ___
3. crypt / tomb   same ___ / different ___

C. Fill in each blank with the correct letter:

a. cryptic	f. circumscribe	k. induce
b. proscribe	g. encrypt	l. conscription
c. mausoleum	h. deduction	m. seduction
d. crypt	i. arcadia	n. cryptography
e. conducive	j. inscription	

1. At the middle of the cemetery stood the grand ___ of the city's wealthiest family.
2. She fended off all his clumsy attempts at ___.
3. She already knew the ___ she wanted on her gravestone: "She done the best she could."
4. She had failed to ___ the file when she put it on her hard drive, and her secretary had secretly copied it.
5. The number of fistfights and accidents at the games had finally forced officials to ___ beer drinking completely.
6. They arrived at the correct conclusion by simple ___.
7. The letter described their new Virginia farm as a kind of ___ of unspoiled nature.
8. He had tried to ___ sleep by all his usual methods, with no success.
9. His answer was so short and ___ that I have no idea what he meant.
10. Their ___ hasn't been revised in two years, and we've been worried about the security of the data.
11. The college feels a strong responsibility for ensuring students' safety, but at the same time it doesn't want to ___ student life too much.
12. Since 1973 there's been no military ___ in the U.S., but that doesn't mean the draft won't come back someday.
13. Conditions on the noisy hallway were not at all ___ to sleep.
14. The great, echoing ___ of St. Stephen's Cathedral could have held hundreds of people.

D. Match the definition on the left to the correct word on the right:

1.	proscribe	a.	deduction
2.	helpful	b.	prohibit
3.	conscription	c.	epitaph
4.	subtraction	d.	induce
5.	circumscribe	e.	conducive
6.	temptation	f.	limit
7.	inscription	g.	seduction
8.	persuade	h.	draft

E. Fill in each blank with the correct letter:

a. cryptic	e. circumscribe	i. conscription
b. induce	f. seduction	j. mausoleum
c. meander	g. proscribe	k. colossus
d. sapphic	h. arcadia	

1. The public isn't aware of the company's ___ of Congress through its huge contributions over many years.
2. One day in the cemetery the ___ door was open, and he peered in with horrified fascination.
3. The only clues for the treasure hunt were in a ___ poem that his father had written.
4. On weekends they would flee to their little ___ in rural New Hampshire, leaving behind the trials of the working week.
5. Military professionals often dislike ___ because most of the recruits don't want to be in the armed services.
6. The paths ___ through the lovely woods, curving back on themselves in long loops.
7. As an experiment, he had written a poem in ___ verse, but he suspected that the rhythm was more suited to Greek.
8. She again told her family that nothing could ___ her to marry him.
9. Occasionally the Congress will try to ___ the president's power, but they usually end up deciding they'd rather not have the new responsibilities themselves.
10. All the states now ___ smoking inside public buildings.
11. The statue for the plaza would be a 30-foot-high ___ representing Atlas holding the globe.

F. Match the definition on the left to the correct word on the right:

1.	inscription	a.	encrypt
2.	lesbian	b.	crypt
3.	translate to code	c.	sapphic
4.	mysterious	d.	prohibit
5.	tomb	e.	cryptic
6.	code writing	f.	dedication
7.	proscribe	g.	cryptography

1. allow : prohibit :: proscribe : ____   a. hesitate b. stick c. permit d. lead

UNIT 37

A. Indicate whether the pairs have the same or different meanings:

1.	endogenous / produced inside	same ___ / different ___
2.	laparoscopy / abdomen examination	same ___ / different ___
3.	lupine / apelike	same ___ / different ___
4.	arthroscopic / insect-viewing	same ___ / different ___
5.	transpire / ooze	same ___ / different ___
6.	oscilloscope / underwater viewer	same ___ / different ___
7.	spirited / energetic	same ___ / different ___
8.	endoscope / electron microscope	same ___ / different ___
9.	endodontic / relating to tooth enamel	same ___ / different ___

B. Fill in each blank with the correct letter:

a. endodontic	d. arthroscopic	g. endorphin
b. oscilloscope	e. endocrine	h. endoscope
c. endogenous	f. laparoscopy	

1. The mechanic always lets her watch the screen of the ____ as he tries to diagnose the sources of her engine's problems.
2. Today there's a specialized type of ____ for looking inside practically every part of the body.
3. This ____ is released in large quantities during serious physical activity and seems to have important painkilling effects.
4. She has always had bad teeth, and now she's finally having ____ work done on the really rotten ones.
5. Low growth rate in teenagers is often an ____ problem that can be fixed with hormones.
6. With ____ surgery, knee operations now take only an hour or so, and the patient leaves the office on crutches soon afterward.
7. The ____ revealed a small stomach tumor, which appeared not to be cancerous.
8. Vitamin d is an ____ vitamin, but bodies seem to require sunlight to produce it.

C. Choose the closest definition:

1. feline   a. sleek   b. clumsy   c. crazy   d. fancy
2. lupine   a. foxy   b. horselike   c. sheepish   d. wolfish

D. Complete the analogy:

1. transfer : hand over :: transpire : ____
   a. breathe out   b. cross   c. encourage   d. come to light
2. gloomy : glum :: spirited : ____
   a. spiraling   b. alcoholic   c. lively   d. complex
3. exciting : thrilling :: dispiriting : ____
   a. dreary   b. calming   c. relaxing   d. soothing
4. pacemaker : heart :: respirator : ____
   a. kidneys   b. brain   c. liver   d. lungs

E. Match the definition on the left to the correct word on the right:

1. leonine   a.   internally produced
2. canine   b.   doglike
3. endogenous   c.   lionlike

F. Fill in each blank with the correct letter:

a. transpire	d. endodontic	g. dispiriting
b. leonine	e. spirited	h. canine
c. respirator	f. feline	

1. Collies and chow chows often have splendid ____ neck ruffs.
2. The dancers, in their black leotards, performed the piece with slinky, ____ grace.
3. The company was doing badly, and she'd been having problems with her boss, so all in all it had been a ____ week at work.
4. There's always a ____ exchange of opinions around the Thanksgiving table, but nobody ever takes offense.
5. Some of the most beloved ____ traits, such as loyalty and playfulness, are often lacking in humans.
6. His father has been living on a ____ for the last two weeks, but now his lungs seem to be improving.
7. Maybe some new information will ____ when they question the family tomorrow.
8. The tooth had been aching for several weeks, but he was still surprised when his dentist told him it would require ____ work.

UNIT 38

A. Fill in each blank with the correct letter:

a. extrapolate	e. muralist	i. intramural
b. avert	f. converter	j. extradite
c. extraneous	g. extrovert	k. bovine
d. revert	h. divert	

1. The last applicant she had interviewed struck her as passive and ____ and completely lacking in ambition.
2. Being a natural ____, he took to his new career as a salesman easily.
3. The college has had an ____ debating society for several years, but this year they've decided to challenge several nearby colleges in a debate competition.
4. She's praying that her daughter doesn't ____ to her old habit of partying several nights a week.
5. The treaty with Brazil doesn't require us to ____ a criminal who's a native-born American.
6. He's locked himself in his studio to ensure that there won't be any ____ distractions.
7. He has a good reputation as a ____ for the wall paintings he's done in public buildings.
8. The generals had discussed what would be involved if they tried to ____ 10,000 troops from Afghanistan to Iraq.
9. From these figures, economists can ____ data that shows a steady increase in employment.
10. Only by seizing a cord dangling beside the window did he manage to ____ disaster.
11. By federal law, every gasoline-powered vehicle must have a catalytic ____ to reduce pollution.

B. Match the definition on the left to the correct word on the right:

1.	avert	b.	go back
2.	immure	c.	seal up
3.	divert	d.	device for adapting
4.	intramural	e.	avoid
5.	porcine	f.	wall painter
6.	revert	g.	entertain
7.	extramural	h.	within an institution
8.	converter	i.	outside an institution
9.	muralist	j.	plump

C. Choose the closest definition:

1.	ovine	a. oval b. egglike c. sheep-related d. birdlike
2.	avert	a. embrace b. prevent c. claim d. escape
3.	caper	a. wolf b. goat c. character d. prank

D. Choose the correct synonym and the correct antonym:

1. divert   a. please   b. entertain   c. bore   d. send
2. avert   a. face   b. wonder   c. avoid   d. claim

E. Indicate whether the pairs have the same or different meanings:

1. extrovert / schizophrenic   same ___ / different ___
2. ovine / goatlike   same ___ / different ___
3. extrapolate / project   same ___ / different ___
4. caper / leap   same ___ / different ___
5. extraneous / necessary   same ___ / different ___
6. immure / embrace   same ___ / different ___
7. extradite / hand over   same ___ / different ___
8. extrapolate / project   same ___ / different ___
9. extraneous / superb   same ___ / different ___
10. extrovert / champion   same ___ / different ___
11. wall up / immure   same ___ / different ___

F. Fill in each blank with the correct letter:

a. muralist   d. immure   g. bovine
b. avert   e. extramural   h. intramural
c. porcine   f. revert

1. Let's not ___ to the kind of name-calling we had to put up with at the last meeting.
2. Her fear of theft was so great that she actually intended to ___ all the gold and silver behind a brick wall in the basement, leaving clues to the location in her will.
3. Nothing ever seemed to disturb her pleasant but ___ manner.
4. They had hired a professional ___ to paint the walls of the staircase with a flowery landscape.
5. The government mental-health center in Washington, D.C., conducts its own research but also funds ___ research at universities across the country.
6. Women's softball was the most popular of the college's ___ sports.
7. She managed to ___ a very awkward meeting by slipping out a side door just as he was coming in.
8. She peeked out to see her ___ landlord climbing the stairs slowly, gasping for breath, with the eviction notice in his hand.

Unit 39

A. Fill in each blank with the correct letter:

a. perspective	e. envisage	i. vulpine
b. vis-à-vis	f. aspect	j. circumvent
c. prospectus	g. visionary	
d. prospect	h. vista	

1. When she considered Cleveland ___ other cities where she might have to live, she always chose Cleveland.
2. The ___ of spending an evening with such an unhappy couple was just depressing.
3. His ambitious plans for the city marked him as a true ___.
4. He had a nervous, ___ manner, with a tense alertness and shifty eyes.
5. The most troubling ___ of the whole incident was the public reaction.
6. The ___ for the new development was full of glowing descriptions that made both of us suspicious.
7. Turning a corner, they found themselves gazing out on the broad ___ of the river valley.
8. Some outside hackers have managed to ___ the country's Internet censorship by clever electronic means.
9. Some judges only look at crimes like these from the ___ of the police.
10. Her therapist keeps asking her if she could ___ getting back together with her husband.

B. Match the definition on the left to the correct word on the right:

1.	compared to	a.	perspective
2.	advance description	b.	envisage
3.	get around	c.	vis-à-vis
4.	prophet	d.	aspect
5.	imagine	e.	prospectus
6.	standpoint	f.	visionary
7.	rim	g.	prospect
8.	outlook	h.	vista
9.	element	i.	asinine
10.	roundabout	j.	circumference
11.	view	k.	circumvent
12.	foolish	l.	circumspect
13.	cautious	m.	circuitous

C. Indicate whether the pairs have the same or different meanings:

1.	equestrian / horselike	same ___ / different ___
2.	circumference / spiral	same ___ / different ___
3.	simian / catlike	same ___ / different ___
4.	circumspect / visible from afar	same ___ / different ___

D. Choose the correct synonym and the correct antonym:

1. visionary   a. idealist   b. cinematographer   c. conservative   d. writer

E. Fill in each blank with the correct letter:

a. circumference	d. asinine	g. circuitous
b. equestrian	e. circumspect	h. vulpine
c. circumvent	f. simian	

1. The child scrambled over the wall with ____ agility.
2. The slick fellow offering his services as guide had a disturbingly ____ air about him.
3. The banking industry generally works hard to ____ any laws that tend to restrict their ability to make profits.
4. Whenever we asked where his income came from, he would say something vague and ____ and treat it as a joke.
5. We finally found the house, but only after getting completely lost and taking an extremely ____ route.
6. They arrived in time to see the top riders compete in the championship ____ event.
7. Jeff and his crowd were in the balcony, catcalling, throwing down cans, and being generally ____.
8. The race course runs the entire ____ of the lake twice, a total of ten miles.

UNIT 40

A. Choose the closest definition:

1. contravene   a. go against   b. retrieve   c. dance   d. object
2. homogeneous   a. self-loving   b. unusually brilliant
                   c. having many parts   d. consistent throughout
3. contraband   a. smuggled goods   b. trade surplus   c. customs   d. imports
4. homologous   a. of different length   b. of similar size
                   c. of different stages   d. of similar origin
5. dictum   a. word   b. statement   c. update   d. answer
6. homogenize   a. treat as the same   b. explain thoroughly
                   c. speak the same language   d. mix thoroughly
7. jurisdiction   a. area of power   b. area of coverage
                   c. area of damage   d. area of target
8. homonym   a. word meaning the same as another
                   b. word spelled and sounded the same as another
                   c. one with same name as another
                   d. one who loves another of the same sex

9. ornithologist   a. student of fish b. student of words
                     c. student of birds d. student of wolves

B. Fill in each blank with the correct letter:

a. edict	c. dictum	e. apiary
b. aquiline	d. jurisdiction	f. diction

1. The farmer tended his ___ lovingly and gathered delicious wildflower honey every year.
2. He often repeated Balzac's famous ___: "Behind every great fortune is a great crime."
3. The judge refused to consider two elements in the case, saying that they lay outside his ___.
4. When their dictatorial grandfather issued an ___, everyone obeyed it.
5. He complains about his students' ___, saying they mumble so much that he often can't understand them.
6. With his ___ nose, he looked like a member of the ancient Roman senate.

C. Match the definition on the left to the correct word on the right:

1. having a consistent texture   a. homologous
2. evolutionarily related   b. homogenize
3. make the same throughout   c. homogeneous
4. word spelled like another   d. homonym

D. Fill in each blank with the correct letter:

a. contraindication	d. contrarian	g. homogeneous
b. edict	e. serpentine	
c. aquiline	f. jurisdiction	

1. Firing local teachers falls outside the superintendant's actual ___.
2. He keeps dinner parties lively with his ___ arguments, which nobody ever agrees with.
3. Proud of the ___ curve of his nose, the star presents his profile to the camera in old silent films at every opportunity.
4. You should blend all ingredients thoroughly to produce a ___ mixture.
5. It was a tall vase, with elaborate ___ shapes winding around it from top to bottom.
6. Pregnancy is a ___ to taking the measles vaccine.
7. The final ___ from the presidential palace commanded every citizen to wear a baseball cap at all times.

E. Indicate whether the pairs have the same or different meanings:

1. homologous / blended   same ___ / different ___
2. contraband / antidote   same ___ / different ___
3. diction / wordiness   same ___ / different ___
4. ornithologist / studier of birds same ___ / different ___

5. contravene / violate   same ___ / different ___
6. dictum / declaration   same ___ / different ___
7. apiary / monkey colony   same ___ / different ___
8. contraindication / benefit   same ___ / different ___
9. jurisdiction / authority   same ___ / different ___
10. serpentine / winding   same ___ / different ___
11. edict / order   same ___ / different ___
12. contrarian / opponent   same ___ / different ___

F. Complete the analogy:

1. accept : oppose :: contravene : ____
   a. go around b. violate c. obey d. distrust
2. opposite : equal :: contrarian : ____
   a. contrast b. conformist c. contradiction d. conflict
3. harm : benefit :: contraindication : ____
   a. denial b. refusal c. injection d. indication
4. idol : adored :: contraband : ____
   a. useful b. opposed c. smuggled d. expensive
5. tolerate : accept :: contravene : ____
   a. argue b. violate c. oppose d. throw out

UNIT 41

A. Choose the closest definition:

1. monotheism   a. nature worship b. worship of one god
                  c. worship of pleasure d. sun worship
2. sophistry   a. deception b. musical composition
                  c. sound reasoning d. pleasure
3. monogamous   a. with one spouse b. without a spouse
                  c. with several spouses d. with someone else's spouse
4. atheistic   a. boring b. godless c. roundabout d. contagious
5. pantheon   a. mall b. road race c. trouser store d. hall of fame

B. Fill in each blank with the correct letter:

a. pantheon   d. panacea   g. apotheosis
b. panoply   e. theocracy   h. pandemonium
c. atheistic   f. pantheism

1. The high priest in this medieval ____ was equivalent to a dictator.

2. Her personal ___ of actresses included Vanessa Redgrave, Helen Mirren, Emma Thompson, and Maggie Smith.
3. His well-known ___ beliefs meant that he couldn't hope for great success in politics.
4. ___ broke out at the news of the victory.
5. Being inducted into the Hall of Fame is as close as a modern ballplayer can come to ___.
6. The new voice-mail system comes with the usual full ___ of options.
7. She had always believed in vitamins as a ___, but they weren't always able to fight off infections.
8. He attended the Presbyterian church, even though for many years his real beliefs had been a mixture of Buddhism and ___.

C. Match the definition on the left to the correct word on the right:

1.	theosophy	a.	immaturely overconfident
2.	panoply	b.	state ruled by religion
3.	pantheon	c.	doctrine of God and the world
4.	sophomoric	d.	nonbelieving
5.	apotheosis	e.	false reasoning
6.	sophistry	f.	hall of fame
7.	theocracy	g.	perfect example
8.	sophisticated	h.	highly complex
9.	atheistic	i.	impressive display

D. Fill in each blank with the correct letter:

a. monotheism	d. pantheism	g. monogamous
b. theocracy	e. monoculture	h. theosophy
c. monolithic	f. apotheosis	

1. The ___ of the great Albert Einstein seemed to occur while he was still living.
2. The relationship was unbalanced: she was perfectly ___, while he had two other women in his life.
3. In a true ___, the legal punishments are often those called for in the holy books.
4. In an old book on ___ she found a philosophy very similar to the one she and her boyfriend were exploring.
5. The sheer mountain face, ___ and forbidding, loomed over the town.
6. Most religious groups in this country practice one or another form of ___.
7. ___ has been a common element in religious belief in the West over many centuries.
8. Corn was a ___ in the village, and the farmers would simply move to a new field each year to keep the soil from wearing out.

E. Indicate whether the pairs have the same or different meanings:

1. pandemonium / uproar   same ___ / different ___

2. monotheism / growing of one crop   same ___ / different ___
3. panacea / antibiotic   same ___ / different ___
4. sophisticated / worldly-wise   same ___ / different ___
5. panoply / display   same ___ / different ___
6. monolithic / boring   same ___ / different ___
7. theosophy / mythology   same ___ / different ___
8. pantheism / priesthood   same ___ / different ___
9. sophistry / wisdom   same ___ / different ___
10. pandemonium / chaos   same ___ / different ___
11. sophomoric / wise   same ___ / different ___
12. panacea / remedy   same ___ / different ___

F. Choose the correct synonym and the correct antonym:

1. sophomoric   a. silly b. wise c. cacophonous d. collegiate
2. sophisticated   a. rejected b. advanced c. worldly-wise d. innocent

UNIT 42

A. Choose the closest synonym:

1. tenet   a. shelter b. principle c. choice d. landlord
2. unilateral   a. one-sided b. sideways c. complete d. multiple
3. tenure   a. strong hold b. permanent appointment
     c. lengthy period d. male voice
4. tenable   a. available b. unbearable c. agreeable d. reasonable
5. unison   a. solitude b. melody c. collection d. agreement
6. tenacious   a. stubborn b. intelligent c. loving d. helping
7. tenet   a. claw b. belief c. renter d. shelter
8. distended   a. overturned b. expired c. swollen d. finished
9. tenuous   a. weak b. sturdy c. contained d. stubborn
10. tenable   a. decent b. tough c. reasonable d. controllable

B. Fill in each blank with the correct letter:

a. unilateral	e. unitarian	i. tact
b. tangible	f. tangential	j. attenuated
c. unison	g. unicameral	
d. tactile	h. extenuating	

1. The question was only ___ to the main subject, but he answered it anyway.
2. The president is allowed to make some ___ decisions without asking Congress's permission.

3.   In rejecting a ____ legislature, America seemed to follow Britain's lead.
4.   She's never had much ____, and her big mouth is always getting her into trouble.
5.   Brain surgeons have highly developed ____ sensitivities.
6.   The district attorney realizes that they don't have much ____ evidence, and he's desperate to dig up more.
7.   As a strict Catholic, she found ____ beliefs unacceptable.
8.   At Halloween and Thanksgiving assemblies, the children would recite holiday poems in ____.
9.   The ____ virus should be incapable of actually causing disease.
10. If you're caught stealing a flat-screen TV, the fact that you can't afford to buy one doesn't count as an ____ circumstance.

C. Match the definition on the left to the correct word on the right:

1.	incidental	a.	tact
2.	politeness	b.	distended
3.	flimsy	c.	attenuated
4.	bulging	d.	extenuating
5.	justifying	e.	tangential
6.	weakened	f.	tenuous

D. Fill in each blank with the correct letter:

a. tenure	d. extenuating	g. tactile
b. attenuated	e. tenacious	h. tenuous
c. intact	f. distended	i. unitarian

1. It was a terrible experience, but they came through it with their sense of humor ____.
2. The dog we used to have bit everyone, and only my mother ever tried to come up with ____ circumstances for his behavior.
3. We used to play with our cousins a lot in our childhood, but all those old friendships have become ____ over the years.
4. He was now yelling, his face red and his veins ____, and I feared he might have a heart attack.
5. The notion of a savior was foreign to his ____ beliefs.
6. The sick child's ____ grip on life was their only hope now.
7. Everyone knows that the ceasefire is ____ and would collapse if one armed soldier decided to go on a rampage.
8. Being blind, his ____ sense was extremely well developed.
9. Their son had just called to tell them that the university had decided to grant him ____.

E. Choose the correct synonym and the correct antonym:

1.   tangible   a. readable b. touchable c. eternal d. nonphysical

F. Indicate whether the pairs have the same or different meanings:

1. tenable / reasonable   same ___ / different ___
2. tenet / ideal   same ___ / different ___
3. unison / unitedness   same ___ / different ___
4. tenure / absence   same ___ / different ___
5. tenacious / sensible   same ___ / different ___
6. tenable / reasonable   same ___ / different ___
7. tangential / touching lightly same ___ / different ___
8. tact / cleverness   same ___ / different ___
9. tactile / sticky   same ___ / different ___
10. unicameral / one-chambered   same ___ / different ___
11. tenet / principle   same ___ / different ___
12. tangible / touchable   same ___ / different ___

UNIT 43

A. Choose the closest definition:

1. metaphorical   a. symbolic b. literary c. descriptive d. extensive
2. duplicity   a. doubleness b. dishonesty c. photocopy d. second opinion
3. metonymy   a. rate of growth b. exaggeration
                     c. model of perfection d. use of a related word
4. morphology   a. study of structure b. study of woods
                     c. study of butterflies d. study of geometry
5. neurotoxin   a. brain wave b. nerve poison c. brain virus d. antidepressant
6. metamorphosis
                     a. condition b. independence c. technique d. transformation

B. Fill in each blank with the correct letter:

a. morphology	e. dimorphic	i. metadata
b. duplex	f. metonymy	j. anthropomorphic
c. metaphysics	g. amorphous	k. dichotomy
d. metamorphosis	h. duplicity	l. metaphorical

1. None of his audio or photo files have any ___ associated with them, so it's impossible to find them via an ordinary Web search.
2. The job description seemed a bit ___, and she wondered what she would really be doing.
3. When the Gypsy Carmen sings "Love is a wild bird," she's being ___.
4. Her poodle really does have some ___ traits, but I'm not sure he really appreciates Beethoven.

5. He seemed to undergo a complete ____ from child to young adult in just a few months.
6. Democracies must always deal with the difficult ____ between individual liberties and social order.
7. He had written his senior thesis on the ____ of a species of dragonfly.
8. Parrots are strikingly ____, unlike canaries, in which you can't tell the sexes apart until the male starts singing.
9. A liar's ____ usually catches up with him sooner or later.
10. They shared the modest ____ with another family of four, who they often met when going in and out.
11. "Green Berets," the nickname for the U.S. Army Special Forces, is a good example of ____.
12. In philosophy he loved ____ most, because it dealt with the deepest mysteries.

C. Choose the correct synonym and the correct antonym:

1. amorphous   a. beginning b. shapeless c. shaping d. formed
2. duplicity   a. desire b. two-facedness c. honesty d. complexity
3. dichotomy   a. operation b. negotiation c. contradiction d. agreement

D. Fill in each blank with the correct letter:

a. anthropomorphic	e. duplex	i. metaphorical
b. toxicity	f. neurotoxin	j. dichotomy
c. metaphysics	g. metamorphosis	k. metadata
d. toxicology	h. toxin	

1. This marble was limestone before it underwent ____.
2. There's so much difficult ____ language in the poem that critics have had a hard time interpreting it.
3. The ____ was roomy, but a great deal of noise came through the wall separating them from the other family.
4. Michelangelo's great painting shows an ____ God touching Adam's finger.
5. Sarin, a manmade ____ 500 times more powerful than cyanide, was outlawed by treaty in 1993.
6. The university offers a graduate degree in environmental ____, which deals with chemical and biological threats to public health.
7. Late-night discussions in the dorm often became arguments about deep topics such as ____.
8. Ricin, a ____ that comes from the castor bean, can be lethal if an amount the size of a grain of sand is inhaled.
9. The ____ between good and evil has been dealt with by different religions in many different ways.
10. The ____ for the photos on his blog site includes identification of every single person in them.
11. Guidebooks warn against the ____ of the water hemlock, the deadliest plant in North America.

E. Indicate whether the pairs have the same or different meanings:

1. morphology / shapeliness   same ___ / different ___
2. toxin / vitamin   same ___ / different ___
3. anthropomorphic / man-shaped   same ___ / different ___
4. toxicity / poisonousness   same ___ / different ___
5. amorphous / shapeless   same ___ / different ___
6. metamorphosis / hibernation   same ___ / different ___

F. Match the definition on the left to the correct word on the right:

1. toxicology   a. poisonousness
2. metonymy   b. equating one thing with another
3. neurotoxin   c. plant-based poison
4. metaphysics   d. nerve poison
5. toxin   e. use of an associated term
6. metaphorical   f. study of the nature of things
7. toxicity   g. information about other information
8. metadata   h. study of poisons

UNIT 44

A. Choose the closest definition:

1. sinecure
   a. hopeful sign   b. unsuccessful search   c. careless act   d. easy job
2. curator   a. doctor   b. lawyer   c. caretaker   d. spectator
3. bipartite   a. double-edged   b. twice-married
   c. two-part   d. having two parties
4. procure   a. say   b. obtain   c. look after   d. heal
5. impart   a. grant   b. stick   c. combine   d. withhold
6. curative   a. purifying   b. healing   c. saving   d. repairing
7. impartial   a. fair   b. biased   c. cautious   d. undecided

B. Indicate whether the pairs have the same or different meanings:

1. impart / give   same ___ / different ___
2. participle / verb part   same ___ / different ___
3. impartial / supportive   same ___ / different ___
4. partisan / fighter   same ___ / different ___

C. Choose the correct synonym and the correct antonym:

1. curative   a. humane   b. unhealthful   c. sensible   d. healing

D. Fill in each blank with the correct letter:

a. bipolar	d. mandatory	g. bipartisan
b. commandeer	e. binary	h. mandate
c. biennial	f. remand	i. sinecure

1. The new bill, with its thoroughly ___ backing, passed through Congress easily.
2. A group of four gunmen tried to ___ the jet soon after takeoff.
3. Powerful drugs like lithium are often prescribed for ___ depression.
4. The court's decision represents a ___ to continue working toward absolute equality in the workplace.
5. At the very heart of the computer revolution was the ___ number system.
6. The judge will probably ___ this case to the lower court for further study.
7. The job turned out to be a ___, and no one cared if he played golf twice a week.
8. The session on business ethics is ___ for all employees.
9. Every two years we get to hear Mildred McDermot sing "Moonlight in Vermont" at the ___ town picnic.

E. Choose the closest definition:

1. curator   a. caretaker b. watcher c. doctor d. purchaser
2. participle   a. verb part b. warning c. supplement d. guerrilla fighter
3. procure   a. appoint b. obtain c. decide d. lose
4. impartial   a. fair b. biased c. accurate d. opinionated
5. bipolar   a. double-jointed b. snowy c. opposing d. two-handed
6. biosphere   a. life cycle b. environment c. natural bubble d. evolution
7. partisan   a. judge b. teacher c. supporter d. leader

F. Fill in each blank with the correct letter:

a. curative	d. biennial	g. curator
b. bipartisan	e. sinecure	h. mandate
c. procure	f. binary	

1. The ___ benefits of antibiotics have saved many lives.
2. The computer works by making choices between ___ opposites.
3. What he had hoped to be an undemanding ___ turned out to be the hardest but most rewarding job of his career.
4. The main piano competition is ___, but there are smaller ones on the off-years.
5. We asked our purchasing manager to ___ new chairs for the office.
6. To keep the issue as nonpolitical as possible, the governor named a ___ committee to study it.
7. The museum's ___ of African art narrates a guided tour of the exhibit.
8. Some politicians claim they have a ___ from the voters even when their margin of victory was actually small.

G. Complete the analogy:

1. donate : contribute :: remand : ____
   a. pass over b. send back c. take on d. give up
2. order : demand :: commandeer : ____
   a. allow b. seize c. rule d. lead

H. Match the definition on the left to the correct word on the right:

1. take over
2. required
3. command
4. send back
5. required
6. participle

a. mandate
b. verb part
c. commandeer
d. mandatory
e. mandatory
f. remand

UNIT 45

A. Choose the closest definition:

1. triad
   a. three-striped flag b. three-headed monster
   c. three-note chord d. three-month delay
2. domination
   a. name b. control c. attraction d. movement
3. trident
   a. three-toothed hag b. three-pronged spear
   c. triple portion d. threesome
4. domineering
   a. owning b. homelike c. royal d. bossy
5. trilogy
   a. three-person conversation b. three-hour nap
   c. three-volume story d. three-ton truck
6. predominant
   a. longest b. lightest c. strongest d. earliest
7. triceratops
   a. three-foot alligator b. three-set tennis match
   c. three-topped tree d. three-horned dinosaur
8. dominion
   a. weakness b. kingdom c. game d. habit

B. Complete the analogy:

1. helpful : servant :: autocratic : ____
   a. friend b. enemy c. teacher d. tyrant
2. persuasion : influence :: domination : ____
   a. household b. country c. command d. outlaw
3. liberty : freedom :: autonomy ____
   a. government b. car science c. independence d. robot
4. obedient : tame :: domineering : ____
   a. sweet b. easygoing c. obnoxious d. controlling

5. immune : infections :: autoimmune : ____
   a. bacteria b. viruses c. epidemic d. body tissues
6. property : estate :: dominion : ____
   a. attitude b. difference c. realm d. country
7. paranoia : suspicion :: autism : ____
   a. sleep b. withdrawal c. anger d. fear of cars
8. larger : smaller :: predominant : ____
   a. secondary b. necessary c. primary d. demanding
9. worker : laborer :: automaton : ____
   a. robot b. computer c. gadget d. employee
10. approval : permission :: autonomy : ____
    a. satisfaction b. independence c. slavery d. poverty

C. Fill in each blank with the correct letter:

a. predominant	d. aristocrat	g. dominion
b. plutocracy	e. trilogy	h. autocratic
c. autonomy	f. bureaucrat	i. automaton

1. She hates being thought of as a ____, but in these huge government offices with long rows of desks it's hard for her to think of herself as anything else.
2. England, though a small nation, once had ____ over a great empire.
3. Her father had been harsh and ____, and her mother and brothers had barely opened their mouths when he was around.
4. When the last volume of her ____ was published, her fans snapped it up eagerly.
5. His parents had been London shopkeepers, but many who met him assumed from his fine manners and accent and dress that he was an ____.
6. She can work like an ____ for eight hours a day, in constant motion, never pausing to speak to a fellow worker.
7. The country is supposedly a democracy, but it's really run as a ____ by about twenty extremely wealthy families.
8. The book was criticized for having too many subjects and no ____ theme.
9. Several remote tribes have been granted limited ____, including self-policing rights and freedom from taxation.

D. Choose the closest definition:

1. autism   a. self-absorption b. self-governance
                 c. authenticity d. authority
2. triad   a. triplet b. chord c. third rail d. three-pointed star
3. bureaucrat   a. furniture maker b. politician c. official d. servant
4. triceratops   a. winged dragon b. dinosaur
                 c. three-part work d. climbing gear
5. aristocrat   a. noble b. power c. ruler d. office worker

E. Indicate whether the pairs have the same or different meanings:

1. automaton / robot   same ____ / different ____
2. autoimmune / invulnerable same ____ / different ____

3. autonomy / freedom   same ___ / different ___
4. autism / dictatorship   same ___ / different ___

F. Match the definition on the left to the correct word on the right:

1. predominant
2. domination
3. plutocracy
4. autocratic
5. bureaucrat
6. aristocrat
7. trident

a. control
b. noble
c. three-pronged spear
d. principal
e. rule by the rich
f. ruled by one person
g. government official

UNIT 46

A. Choose the closest definition:

1. omnivore   a. world traveler b. meat- and plant-eater
   c. universe d. bottom-feeder
2. trimester   a. a three-cornered hat b. a period of about three months
   c. a three-masted sailing ship d. a three-minute egg
3. omnipotent   a. almighty b. all-knowing c. all-seeing d. all-round
4. trivial   a. crossed b. indented c. unimportant d. found
5. omniscient   a. immense b. all-knowing c. universal d. unlimited
6. trinity   a. romantic triangle b. three-part recipe
   c. group of three d. triplets
7. omnibus   a. immense b. transporting c. all-inclusive d. worldwide
8. triptych   a. three-week travel voucher b. three-part painting
   c. three-phase rocket d. three-handed clock
9. carnage   a. meat b. slaughter c. flesh d. battle
10. voracious   a. vast b. hungry c. fierce d. unsatisfied

B. Indicate whether the pairs have the same or different meanings:

1. carnage / slaughter   same ___ / different ___
2. insectivorous / buglike   same ___ / different ___
3. reincarnation / rebirth   same ___ / different ___
4. voracious / extremely hungry   same ___ / different ___
5. carnal / spiritual   same ___ / different ___
6. herbivorous / vegetarian   same ___ / different ___
7. incarnate / holy   same ___ / different ___
8. carnivorous / meat-eating   same ___ / different ___

9. trimester / school-year term   same ___ / different ___
10. trinity / group of three   same ___ / different ___

C. Complete the analogy:

1. educated : unschooled :: omniscient : ___
    a. commanding b. lazy c. ignorant d. know-it-all
2. fiduciary : trust-based :: carnivorous : ___
    a. vegetarian b. meat-eating c. greedy d. hungry
3. selective : limited :: omnibus : ___
    a. everyday b. all-time c. oversized d. comprehensive
4. insectivorous : insects :: herbivorous : ___
    a. plants b. herbs c. grains d. flowers
5. weak : feeble :: omnipotent : ___
    a. timid b. all-powerful c. global d. huge
6. carnage : bloodbath :: Penelope : ___
    a. wife b. mother c. daughter d. siren
7. human : deer :: omnivore : ___
    a. plant-eater b. elk c. ape d. dieter

D. Fill in each blank with the correct letter:

a. reincarnation	e. voracious	i. plutocracy
b. insectivorous	f. herbivorous	j. trivial
c. carnage	g. carnal	k. autocratic
d. carnivorous	h. incarnate	

1. Sheep, cattle, and antelope are ___; unlike dogs and cats, they show no interest in meat.
2. The school tried to shield students from ___ temptations.
3. The smallest mammal is the bumblebee bat, an ___ creature about the size of a dime.
4. Today he speaks of his former stepfather as evil ___, and his mother doesn't argue with him.
5. From the variety of books on his shelves, we could tell he was a ___ reader.
6. She constantly assured her employees that their opinions were never ___ or unimportant.
7. Even the ambulance drivers were horrified by the ___ of the accident.
8. The ___ that controls the government also controls all the country's news media.
9. As a child she loved to watch them throw meat to the ___ ones, especially the lions and tigers.
10. The current Dalai Lama is said to be the 13th ___ of the first one, who lived in the 15th century.
11. Replacing an ___ government with a democracy is never easy if the country is unfamiliar with democratic procedures.

A. 1.d 2.b 3.a 4.c 5.b 6.c 7.c 8.b 9.b 10.b
B. 1.s 2.d 3. 4.s 5.a 6.s 7.d 8.e 9.e 10.a C. 1.c 2.b 3.d 4.a 5.b 6.a 7.a
D. 1.f 2.g 3.b 4.h 5.e 6.j 7.c 8.i 9.d 10.a 11.x

UNIT 47

A. Choose the closest definition:

1. docent   a. leader b. scholar c. guide d. minister
2. pedestrian   a. useless b. footlike c. unusual d. boring
3. pedagogy   a. study b. teaching c. research d. child abuse
4. doctrine   a. solution b. principle c. religion d. report
5. impediment   a. help b. obstacle c. footpath d. obligation
6. doctrinaire   a. by the way b. by the by c. by the rule d. by the glass
7. pedigree   a. wealth b. education c. breeding d. purity
8. indoctrinate   a. teach b. demonstrate c. infiltrate d. consider

B. Match the definition on the left to the correct word on the right:

1.	thorough	a.	quadriplegic
2.	boring teacher	b.	pediatrician
3.	education	c.	quadrant
4.	children's doctor	d.	encyclopedic
5.	guide	e.	quartile
6.	fill with a point of view	f.	pedant
7.	ancestry	g.	indoctrinate
8.	official teaching	h.	pedagogy
9.	rigidly principled	i.	docent
10.	one-fourth of a group	j.	doctrine
11.	paralyzed in four limbs	k.	impediment
12.	ordinary	l.	quadruped
13.	quarter	m.	pedestrian
14.	formal dance	n.	pedigree
15.	obstacle	o.	doctrinaire
16.	four-footed animal	p.	quadrille

C. Indicate whether the pairs have the same or different meanings:

1. pedagogy / teaching   same ___ / different ___
2. encyclopedic / important   same ___ / different ___
3. pediatrician / foot doctor   same ___ / different ___
4. pedant / know-it-all   same ___ / different ___
5. quadrille / square dance   same ___ / different ___

D. Choose the correct synonym and the correct antonym:

1. doctrinaire   a. relaxed b. strict c. written d. religious

E. Fill in each blank with the correct letter:

a. doctrinaire	e. quadriplegic	i. encyclopedic
b. pedigree	f. impediment	j. doctrine
c. pedant	g. pediatrician	k. quartile
d. pedestrian	h. quadruped	

1. The presence of her little sister was a definite ___ to her romantic plans for the evening.
2. Tuesday the baby sees the ___ for her immunizations and checkups.
3. As a practicing Catholic, she thought frequently about the church ___ that life begins at conception.
4. By the time she was 25 she had an ___ knowledge of her state's history.
5. Because of technological advances and access laws, the life of a ___ is far less restricted than it once was.
6. From his fleeting glimpse, all he could tell was that it was a small brown ___ that could move very fast.
7. A ___ interpretation of these rules will leave no room for fun at all.
8. At the age of 72 he was regarded by most of the students as a boring ___.
9. A grade-point average that falls in the top ___ earns a student special privileges.
10. His sister's trips to Borneo made his vacations at the seashore seem ___.
11. His rather snobbish grandmother only seemed to be concerned about his fiancée's ___.

F. Complete the analogy:

1. ambivalent : uncertain :: pedestrian : ___
   a. slow b. colorful c. unexciting d. explosive

UNIT 48

A. Match the definition on the left to the correct word on the right:

1.	four-sided solid	a.	configuration
2.	arrangement	b.	tetralogy
3.	antibiotic	c.	tetracycline
4.	four connected works	d.	tetrapod
5.	four-limbed animal	e.	tetrahedron

B. Indicate whether the pairs have the same or different meanings:

1.	formative / form-giving	same ___ / different ___
2.	figment / fruitcake	same ___ / different ___

3.	conform / agree	same ___ / different ___
4.	figurative / mathematical	same ___ / different ___
5.	format / arrangement	same ___ / different ___
6.	effigy / bonfire	same ___ / different ___
7.	formality / convention	same ___ / different ___
8.	configuration / list of parts	same ___ / different ___
9.	four-part work / tetralogy	same ___ / different ___

C. Fill in each blank with the correct letter:

a. figurative	d. format	g. configuration
b. formative	e. figment	h. formality
c. effigy	f. conform	

1. No one was surprised when WTFX's new ___ turned out to be exactly the same as that of the company's 70 other stations.
2. The ___ of the new aircraft's wings was one of the Defense Department's most closely held secrets.
3. While on the base, visitors are expected to ___ with all official rules and regulations.
4. Don't tell him, but his popularity is just a ___ of his imagination.
5. He only meant the remark in a ___ sense, but lots of people thought he meant it literally.
6. The new couple found the ___ of the elegant dinner a little overwhelming.
7. Among her ___ influences she included her favorite uncle, her ballet classes, and the Nancy Drew series.
8. Every Halloween they would set a crude ___ of a farmer on their porch, though they never really knew why.

D. Choose the closest definition:

1.	longueur	a. couch b. distance c. boring section d. length
2.	format	a. design b. formality c. formation d. concept
3.	elongate	a. continue b. smooth over c. close off d. lengthen
4.	indoctrinate	a. medicate thoroughly b. research thoroughly
		c. instruct thoroughly d. consider thoroughly

E. Choose the correct synonym and the correct antonym:

1.	formality	a. convention b. black tie c. rationality d. casualness
2.	figurative	a. modeled b. literal c. painted d. symbolic
3.	conform	a. rebel b. shape c. greet d. fit in

F. Fill in each blank with the correct letter:

a. figment	e. elongate	i. tetrahedron
b. longitude	f. tetracycline	j. formative
c. tetrapod	g. conform	k. longueur
d. effigy	h. oblong	

1. By following a few basic tips, you can ___ your laptop battery's life by a month or more.
2. Penicillin and ___ are among the most useful of the antibiotics.
3. We failed to get the contract because our equipment didn't ___ to the company's specifications.
4. Every large land animal is a ___, as is every bird.
5. The shields used by Celtic warriors were ___ rather than round, and thus able to protect much of the body.
6. The talk was just one ___ after another, and she finally got up and tiptoed out of the lecture hall.
7. The idea that my parents don't like you is a ___ of your imagination.
8. A ___ can be a strong and stable structure, since it's made of four triangles.
9. The assignment was to write an essay about the most ___ experience of her later teenage years.
10. For the homecoming celebration, we made an ___ of our opponents' mascot and draped it in black.
11. Even the Greeks knew how to calculate latitude from the sun and stars, but no one managed to measure ___ accurately until the 18th century.

UNIT 49

A. Choose the closest definition:

1. negligible   a. small b. correctable c. noteworthy d. considerate
2. critique   a. mystique b. commentary c. argument d. defense
3. negligent   a. penniless b. careless c. criminal d. decent
4. hypercritical   a. pretended b. complimentary
   c. underdeveloped d. overly harsh
5. abnegation   a. abundance b. abruptness
   c. self-denial d. self-satisfaction
6. criterion   a. dinosaur b. mourning c. criticism d. gauge
7. renege   a. repeat b. go back on c. renegotiate d. overturn

B. Indicate whether the pairs have the same or different meanings:

1. hematocrit / test tube   same ___ / different ___
2. negligible / ignorable   same ___ / different ___
3. hypercritical / untruthful   same ___ / different ___
4. abnegation / absence   same ___ / different ___
5. criterion / standard   same ___ / different ___
6. negligent / neglectful   same ___ / different ___
7. critique / evaluation   same ___ / different ___

8. renege / return   same ___ / different ___
9. negligible / unimportant same ___ / different ___
10. prescient/ foresighted   same ___ / different ___

C. Match the definition on the left to the correct word on the right:

1. prescient   a. having foresight
2. Pentateuch   b. first books of the Bible
3. nescience   c. lack of knowledge
4. pentathlon   d. event with five contests
5. unconscionable   e. evangelically Christian
6. Pentecostal   f. careful
7. conscientious   g. inexcusable
8. pentameter   h. poetic rhythm

D. Complete the analogy:

1. clever : brainy :: prescient : ___
    a. evil b. wise c. existing d. painstaking
2. informed : ignorant :: conscientious : ___
    a. careful b. all-seeing c. well-informed d. scientific
3. data : information :: nescience : ___
    a. wisdom b. ignorance c. judgment d. learning
4. corrupt : honest :: unconscionable : ___
    a. orderly b. attractive c. universal d. moralc. conscientious

E. Fill in each blank with the correct letter:

        a. hematocrit   d. prescient   g. critique
        b. pentathlon   e. hypercritical   h. conscientious
        c. criterion   f. Pentecostal

1. He had never learned how to make his criticism seem constructive rather
    than ___.
2. The most successful stockbrokers have the reputation of being almost
    eerily ___.
3. The judges gave a thorough and helpful ___ of each contestant's work.
4. They grew up attending a ___ church, watching their father speak in
    tongues on most Sundays.
5. What shall we use as the basic ___ for this award?
6. She won praise for her ___ handling of details.
7. The ___ showed an abnormal ratio of red blood cells.
8. Track stars with superb all-round training usually try out for the ___
    competition.

F. Choose the closest definition:

1. renege   a. afford b. honor c. flee d. deny
2. Pentateuch   a. New Testament books b. five-sided figure
                  c. Old Testament books d. five-pointed star

3. abnegation   a. position   b. self-indulgence   c. self-denial   d. refusal
4. pentameter   a. five-line stanza   b. five-word sentence
                   c. five-beat poetic line   d. five-sided shape
5. criterion   a. argument   b. scolding   c. standard   d. critical review
6. pentathlon   a. five competitions   b. five-note scale
                   c. five-month period   d. five-sided figure

UNIT 50

A. Choose the closest definition:

1. regency   a. monarch   b. acting government   c. crowning   d. royal style
2. quintile   a. fifteenth   b. five-spot   c. group of five   d. one fifth
3. regimen   a. army unit   b. dynasty   c. rule book   d. routine
4. quintessential   a. fifth   b. being   c. ideal   d. important
5. interregnum   a. vacation   b. recess
                   c. period without a leader   d. period of peace
6. quincentennial   a. 5th anniversary   b. 15th anniversary
                   c. 50th anniversary   d. 500th anniversary
7. regalia   a. royalty   b. set of rules
                   c. training schedule   d. trappings of office
8. legate   a. heritage   b. gift   c. ambassador   d. letter

B. Match the definition on the left to the correct word on the right:

1.	agent	a.	transmission
2.	errand	b.	quintile
3.	sending	c.	quintet
4.	evangelist	d.	mission
5.	most typical	e.	quincentennial
6.	500th birthday	f.	missionary
7.	one fifth of a group	g.	quintessential
8.	composition for five	h.	emissary

C. Complete the analogy:

1. habit : custom :: legacy : ____
    a. descendant   b. tradition   c. transit   d. deputy
2. governor : executive :: legate : ____
    a. letter   b. priest   c. deputy   d. bandit
3. flock : group of sheep :: delegation : ____
    a. group of candidates   b. group of worshippers
    c. group of runners   d. group of representatives

4. revise : amend :: relegate : ____
   a. vanish b. banish c. tarnish d. varnish
5. present : gift :: legacy : ____
   a. ownership b. legal settlement c. will d. inheritance

D. Fill in each blank with the correct letter:

a. mission	e. regency	i. legacy
b. regimen	f. critique	j. emissary
c. criterion	g. missionary	k. interregnum
d. transmission	h. regalia	

1. At a ceremonial occasion such as this, every officer would be present, in full ____.
2. Each generation hopes to leave the next a ____ of peace and prosperity.
3. Every pope's death is followed by a short ____ while the cardinals prepare to choose a new pope.
4. ____ of the bacteria usually occurs through close personal contact.
5. His 20-year-old daughter took over the company when he died, but her first couple of years were really a ____ under the senior vice president.
6. The only people in the village who could speak English were a Peace Corps volunteer and a ____ at the little church.
7. Her new ____ included a yoga session and a one-hour bike ride every day.
8. Their ____ on this occasion was to convince their elderly father to surrender his driver's license.
9. An ____ was sent to the Duke with a new offer.
10. He would write a lengthy ____ on every term paper, though he suspected few of the students ever read them.
11. Her main ____ for a boyfriend was a great sense of humor.

E. Choose the closest definition:

1. regimen   a. daily plan b. strict order c. ruling family d. officers' club
2. regalia   a. monarchy b. official costume c. regularity d. solemn dignity
3. mission   a. greeting b. assignment c. support d. departure

F. Fill in each blank with the correct letter:

a. transmission	e. quintessential	i. hematocrit
b. relegate	f. legacy	j. quintile
c. regency	g. quintet	
d. delegation	h. legate	

1. She's having her bloodwork done and is waiting anxiously to hear her ____.
2. The king's ____ arrived two weeks early in order to negotiate the agreement that the king would later sign in person.
3. The test results placed her in the highest ____ of the population.
4. The government is struggling to overcome a ____ of corruption that goes back a hundred years or more.

5. For her, *The Night of the Living Dead* remained the ___ horror film, against which she judged all the others.
6. At the conference a carefully chosen ___ presented its views to the president.
7. The concert ended with a string ___ by Beethoven.
8. There in the corner, where the shopkeeper had decided to ___ him, sat a stuffed bear with a mournful face.
9. ___ of electric power over long distances always involves considerable losses.
10. The ___ lasted several years, as the boy king passed through an awkward preadolescent stage to emerge as a serious and dignified 20-year-old.

UNIT 51

A. Choose the closest definition:

1. compel   a. drive b. prevent c. eject d. compare
2. diminutive   a. little b. cozy c. detailed d. comfortable
3. repel   a. attract b. greet c. offend d. send
4. minutiae   a. particles b. leftovers c. moments d. trivia
5. decimate   a. destroy b. pair up c. multiply d. remove

B. Match the definition on the left to the correct word on the right:

1.	force by moral pressure	a.	enumerate
2.	disgust	b.	compel
3.	drive out	c.	repel
4.	combining numbers and letters	d.	minutiae
5.	list	e.	expel
6.	extra	f.	diminutive
7.	small	g.	impel
8.	details	h.	alphanumeric
9.	drive irresistibly	i.	supernumerary
10.	miniature	j.	minimalism
11.	occult use of numbers	k.	minuscule
12.	style of extreme simplicity	l.	numerology

C. Indicate whether the pairs have the same or different meanings:

1. enumerate / solve   same ___ / different ___
2. minuscule / empty   same ___ / different ___
3. decalogue / set of rules   same ___ / different ___

4. supernumerary / extra   same ___ / different ___
5. list / enumerate   same ___ / different ___
6. impel / cause to act   same ___ / different ___

D. Fill in each blank with the correct letter:

a. expel	e. decathlon	i. compel
b. decimate	f. impel	j. decibel
c. supernumerary	g. decalogue	
d. repel	h. minimalism	

1. They knew that hunger would eventually ___ the grizzly to wake up.
2. No one bothers to compete in the ___ who isn't an extraordinary natural athlete.
3. Men like him normally ___ her, so I'm surprised that she seems interested.
4. The ___ in the Old Testament is matched by the Beatitudes in the New Testament.
5. Though the Senate can ___ a member for certain crimes, it's almost never been done.
6. An earthquake can easily ___ the buildings of an entire city.
7. Don't count on conscience to ___ most people to make the right choice under such difficult circumstances.
8. The ear can usually hear the difference between noises that differ in intensity by a single ___.
9. Only six people could play on a side, so the ___ volleyball players had to wait five minutes before rotating into the game.
10. The critics call her novels good examples of ___, since she barely describes people or scenes at all and the action is never really explained.

E. Fill in each blank with the correct letter:

a. supernumerary	e. diminutive	i. decibel
b. minimalism	f. decathlon	j. numerology
c. expel	g. alphanumeric	k. minuscule
d. enumerate	h. minutiae	

1. He enjoys working on actual cases, but he gets worn down by the flood of ___ involved in billing his clients.
2. For his annual salary review, his boss always asks him to ___ the projects he completed during the previous year.
3. She's a big fan of ___ in Web design, and Google's white home page has always been her ideal.
4. As a child, she had a couple of ___ teeth, which the dentist pulled when she was 8 years old.
5. That music might sound better if the sound were turned down a ___ or two.
6. She can't stand it when they start arguing over ___ differences while ignoring the really important issues.

7. She occasionally visited a local fortune-teller, who would use playing cards and ____ to predict her future.
8. The Web site uses six-character ____ passwords, of which there are enough for tens of millions of users.
9. Which of the ten events in the ____ is your favorite?
10. The archerfish can ____ sudden jets of water at insects, knocking them into the lake or river.
11. People often comment on the contrast between his ____ physique and the enormous power he wields on Capitol Hill.

UNIT 52

A. Choose the closest definition:

1. longevity   a. extent b. life length c. longitude d. longing
2. temporal   a. religious b. ideal c. time-related d. durable
3. coeval   a. ancient b. simultaneous c. same-sized d. continuing
4. anachronism   a. electronic clock b. literary theory
                    c. misplacement in time d. current topic
5. medieval   a. antiquated b. middle-aged c. romantic d. knightly
6. primeval   a. wicked b. elderly c. primitive d.muddy

B. Match the definition on the left to the correct word on the right:

1. temporal   a. current
2. synchronous   b. order of events
3. medieval   c. ongoing
4. temporize   d. happening at the same time
5. anachronism   e. talk to fill time
6. longevity   f. improvised
7. extemporaneous   g. measurable by time
8. chronic   h. misplacement in time
9. primeval   i. of the same age
10. contemporary   j. of the Middle Ages
11. chronology   k. length of life
12. coeval   l. ancient

C. Indicate whether the pairs have the same or different meanings:

1. centimeter / 1/1000 of a meter   same ___ / different ___
2. chronology / order of events   same ___ / different ___

D. Choose the correct synonym and the correct antonym:

1. longevity   a. anniversary   b. shortness   c. uncertainty   d. permanence
2. primeval   a. recent   b. antique   c. ancient   d. swamplike

E. Complete the analogy:

1. antique : ancient :: contemporary : ____
   a. simultaneous   b. modern   c. fragile   d. warped
2. drama : scenes :: chronology : ____
   a. events   b. clock   c. length   d. sequence
3. argue : agree :: temporize : ____
   a. discuss   b. negotiate   c. conclude   d. grow cold
4. infrequent : occasional :: chronic : ____
   a. short   b. surprising   c. continuous   d. noisy
5. sudden : expected :: extemporaneous : ____
   a. sudden   b. rehearsed   c. off-the-cuff   d. off-the-wall
6. foreigner : country :: anachronism : ____
   a. antique   b. novelty   c. watch   d. time period
7. temporary : enduring :: temporal : ____
   a. modern   b. existing   c. arising   d. eternal
8. amorphous : shapeless :: synchronous : ____
   a. simultaneous   b. in sequence   c. out of order   d. always late

F. Fill in each blank with the correct letter:

a. centurion	e. synchronous	i. contemporary
b. coeval	f. extemporaneous	j. medieval
c. temporize	g. centimeter	k. chronic
d. centigrade	h. centenary	

1. Several other great Dutch artists were ____ with Rembrandt.
2. The company celebrated its ____ this month, and one of the founder's elderly children was able to come.
3. In ____ Europe, great walls were erected around entire cities for the protection of the people.
4. For high-school dancers, their movements were remarkably ____.
5. Rain is likely to become snow at about 0° ____.
6. The legion commanders decided that each ____ should divide up the food within his own century.
7. The doctor told him his condition was ____ and untreatable but not life-threatening.
8. Having left his notes at home, he had to give an entirely ____ lecture.
9. That tree was planted when I was born, so it and I are ____.
10. No matter how long you ____ and stall for time, the problem won't go away.
11. Last week's rainfall in Paris measured less than a ____.

UNIT 53

A. Choose the closest definition:

1. aver   a. reject b. detract c. deny d. assert
2. verify   a. reverse b. mislead c. prove d. test

B. Fill in each blank with the correct letter:

a. simulacrum	e. verify	i. centenary
b. aver	f. kilometer	j. assimilate
c. centurion	g. simile	k. veracity
d. simulate	h. verisimilitude	

1. The ___ and his soldiers had proved themselves skilled fighters in the battles on the eastern frontier.
2. Most students can't ___ so much information all at once, so they approach it gradually.
3. The prosecutor expected the witness to ___ that the suspect was guilty.
4. Critics complained about the lack of ___ in his crime writing, saying it sounded as if he'd never even been inside a police station.
5. A ___ is more than half a mile but less than two-thirds of a mile.
6. My grandfather celebrates his ___ in May.
7. She was never able to ___ anything he had told her about his past.
8. The boys claim they never went near the river that afternoon, but we suspect their ___.
9. That restaurant doesn't offer real maple syrup, just an unconvincing ___.
10. She did her best to ___ pleasure at the news, but could barely manage a smile.
11. "A day without sunshine is like a chicken without a bicycle" has to be the oddest ___ of all time.

C. Indicate whether the pairs have the same or different meanings:

1. sensuous / sensitive   same ___ / different ___
2. verify / prove   same ___ / different ___
3. extrasensory / extreme   same ___ / different ___
4. aver / claim   same ___ / different ___
5. desensitize / deaden   same ___ / different ___
6. sensor / scale   same ___ / different ___
7. kilohertz / unit of frequency   same ___ / different ___
8. pounds / kilogram   same ___ / different ___

D. Match the definition on the left to the correct word on the right:

1.	kilobyte	b.	3/5 of a mile
2.	extrasensory	c.	detector
3.	kilogram	d.	measure of electronic capacity
4.	assimilate	e.	pleasing to the senses
5.	sensuous	f.	1,000 vibrations per second
6.	kilohertz	g.	not using the senses
7.	simulacrum	h.	2.2 pounds
8.	desensitize	i.	absorb
9.	kilometer	j.	make numb
10.	sensor	k.	replica

E. Complete the analogy:

1. extent : length :: simile : ____
   a. shape b. contrast c. kind d. comparison
2. believe : doubt :: aver : ____
   a. state b. mean c. deny d. subtract
3. inflate : expand :: simulate : ____
   a. reveal b. entrap c. devote d. imitate
4. illusion : fantasy :: verisimilitude : ____
   a. appearance b. realism c. style d. proof
5. create : invent :: assimilate : ____
   a. wring b. absorb c. camouflage d. drench
6. praise : ridicule :: verify : ____
   a. testify b. contradict c. establish d. foretell
7. painting : portrays :: simulacrum : ____
   a. imitates b. shows c. demonstrates d. calculates
8. loyalty : treason :: veracity : ____
   a. dishonesty b. truthfulness c. ideals d. safekeeping
9. deceive : mislead :: simulate : ____
   a. increase b. excite c. grow d. imitate
10. contrast : different :: simile : ____
   a. near b. distant c. alike d. clear

F. Fill in each blank with the correct letter:

a. kilogram	e. extrasensory	i. simile
b. sensuous	f. veracity	j. kilometer
c. verisimilitude	g. kilobyte	
d. kilohertz	h. desensitize	

1. Every Tuesday there's a 5-____ race along the river, which is short enough that 10-year-olds sometimes run it.
2. After a month of barefoot running, he had managed to thoroughly ____ the soles of his feet.
3. On a hard drive, a ____ is enough capacity for a few sentences of text, but for audio or video it's too small to even mention.

4. The defense lawyers knew the jury might be doubtful about the next witness's ___.
5. The broadcast frequencies of FM stations are required to be 200 ___ apart so as not to interfere with each other.
6. When they first moved to Berlin, it took them a few days to get used to buying potatoes and oranges by the ___ rather than the pound.
7. Her films showed her own reality, and she had no interest in ___.
8. The worst ___ in the song is the one that compares his beloved to a really solid six-cylinder engine.
9. She lay in the bath with her eyes closed in a kind of ___ daydream.
10. Husband and wife seemed to communicate by ___ means, each always guessing what the other needed before anything was said.

A. 1.d 2.c B. 1.c 2.j 3.b 4.h 5.f 6.i 7.e 8.k 9.a 10.d 11.g C. 1.d 2.s 3.d 4.e 5.e 6.d 7.a 8.a D. 1.c 2.f 3.g 4.h 5.d 6.e 7.j 8.i 9.a 10.b E. 1.d 2.c 3.d 4.b 5.b 6.b 7.a 8.a 9.d 10.c F. 1.j 2.h 3.g 4.f 5.d 6.a 7.c 8.i 9.b 10.e

UNIT 54

A. Choose the closest definition:

1.	precision	a. accuracy b. beauty c. brilliance d. dependence
2.	perennial	a. flowerlike b. excellent c. everlasting d. thorough
3.	sanction	a. pray b. warn c. trade d. approve
4.	excise	a. add b. examine c. refuse d. cut out
5.	superannuated	a. amazing b. huge c. aged d. perennial
6.	sacrosanct	a. sacred b. churchlike c. Christian d. priestly
7.	incisive	a. damaging b. sharp c. lengthy d. definite
8.	millennium	a. thousand b. century c. era d. a thousand years
9.	sanctimonious	a. hypocritical b. holy c. solemn d. divine
10.	concise	a. concentrated b. sure c. shifting d. blunt
11.	annuity	a. annual event b. annual payment c. annual income d. annual garden
12.	sanctuary	a. belief b. holiness c. cemetery d. refuge
13.	millipede	a. thousand-year blight b. many-legged arthropod c. hundred million d. obstacle

B. Indicate whether the pairs have the same or different meanings:

1.	sanction / dedicate	same ___ / different ___
2.	sacrosanct / heavenly	same ___ / different ___
3.	sanctuary / shelter	same ___ / different ___
4.	sanctimonious / passionate	same ___ / different ___
5.	annuity / yearly payment	same ___ / different ___

C. Fill in each blank with the correct letter:

a. millennium	d. precision	g. superannuated
b. concise	e. millenarianism	h. incisive
c. millefleur	f. excise	

1. Ms. Raymond's report was ___ but managed to discuss all the issues.
2. The year 2000 marked the start of the third ___.
3. Since everyone interprets the Bible's prophecies differently, ___ has broken out at many different times through the centuries.
4. The judge was deeply knowledgeable about the case, and his questions to both lawyers were ___.
5. A design with a detailed ___ background is a challenge for even a needlepoint expert.
6. She knows that creaky old chair is ___, but she loves it and wouldn't give it up for anything.
7. Before eating an apple, some people carefully ___ the brown spots.
8. What the tipsy darts players lacked in ___ they made up for in enthusiasm.

D. Choose the correct synonym and the correct antonym:

1. perennial   a. two-year   b. lasting   c. temporary   d. flowering

E. Choose the correct *antonym*:

1. incisive   a. dull   b. noble   c. faulty   d. exceptional
2. concise   a. lengthy   b. wide   c. dated   d. brief

F. Match the definition on the left to the correct word on the right:

1.	era of earthly paradise	a.	perennial
2.	worn out	b.	sanctimonious
3.	continuing	c.	annuity
4.	regular payment	d.	millennium
5.	hypocritical	e.	superannuated

G. Fill in each blank with the correct letter:

a. gastrectomy	e. mastectomy	i. precision
b. millefleur	f. sacrosanct	j. millipede
c. appendectomy	g. tonsillectomy	
d. millisecond	h. millenarianism	

1. ___ increased dramatically as the year 2000 approached.
2. After her ___ the breast had been completely reconstructed.
3. The poison from the largest tropical centipedes can be lethal to small children, but a ___ could never kill a human.
4. He had undergone a ___ after tests had revealed tumors on the stomach wall.
5. For the baby's room they chose wallpaper with a dainty ___ design.
6. I myself had a ___ when I was 11, but my son's tonsils got better after a week of antibiotics.

7. We set the clock with great ___ on the first day of every new year.
8. Under the new boss, no department here is ___ and almost any of them could be broken up tomorrow.
9. Some Olympic races have been extremely close, but no one has ever won by a single ___.
10. X-rays showed that the appendix was badly swollen, and they managed to schedule an ___ for that same afternoon.

H. Complete the analogy:

1. church : temple :: sanctuary : ___
   a. destination b. parish c. destiny d. refuge
2. milliliter : volume :: millisecond : ___
   a. distance b. weight c. time d. mass
3. release : restrain :: sanction : ___
   a. disapprove b. request c. train d. decide

UNIT 55

A. Choose the closest definition:

1. impose   a. force b. request c. seek d. hint
2. prerequisite   a. pattern b. requirement c. preference d. direction
3. superimpose   a. surpass b. put into c. place over d. amaze
4. predispose   a. recycle b. eliminate c. demonstrate d. influence
5. juxtapose   a. place on top of b. put away
                   c. place side by side d. put into storage
6. preclude   a. come before b. come after c. prevent d. predict
7. transpose   a. emerge b. change into c. cross d. switch
8. precocious   a. nearly cooked b. maturing early
                   c. self-contradictory d. necessary
9. excise   a. call out b. hold out c. cut out d. fold out

B. Complete the analogy:

1. spendthrift : thrifty :: acquisitive : ___
   a. wealthy b. uncertain c. curious d. unselfish
2. paraplegia : legs :: hemiplegia : ___
   a. paralysis b. stroke c. lungs d. left or right side
3. prefer : favor :: preclude : ___
   a. assume b. expect c. prevent d. avoid

C. Fill in each blank with the correct letter:

a. semicolon	f. acquisitive	k. prerequisite
b. preclude	g. hemiplegia	l. inquisition
c. requisition	h. precocious	m. impose
d. semitone	i. perquisite	
e. predispose	j. semiconductor	

1. A childhood disease had resulted in the crippling ___ that had confined him to a wheelchair for ten years.
2. At 13 she was ___ enough to mingle with the guests at her parents' cocktail parties.
3. Everything I had heard about the guy from my friends didn't exactly ___ me to like him.
4. Seeing that the highest note was out of her comfortable range, she asked her pianist to play the whole song a ___ lower.
5. The whole family was ___ by nature, and there were bitter legal battles over the will.
6. The legislature is threatening to ___ strict limits on this kind of borrowing.
7. His status as newcomer did carry the special ___ of being able to ask a lot of questions.
8. Louisa feared an ___ into her background and previous involvements.
9. You couldn't even get a pencil unless you filled out a ___.
10. In most integrated circuits, silicon is used as the ___.
11. The meaning of a clause rarely depends on whether it ends with a colon or a ___.
12. Any felony conviction in your past would ___ your getting a job with the state government.
13. The only ___ for taking the Galaxies course is a strong background in high-school math and physics.

D. Indicate whether the pairs have the same or different meanings:

1. impose / remove   same ___ / different ___
2. inquisition /curiosity   same ___ / different ___
3. transpose / exchange   same ___/ different ___
4. requisition / requirement   same ___/ different ___
5. superimpose / offend deeply   same ___ / different ___
6. acquisitive / greedy   same ___ / different ___
7. juxtapose / switch   same ___ / different ___
8. perquisite / salary   same ___ / different ___
9. acquisitive / generous   same ___ / different ___

E. Choose the closest definition:

1. semicolon   a. small intestine   b. punctuation mark c. low hill   d. small bush
2. predispose   a. recycle   b. subdue   c. spread   d. influence
3. precocious   a. previous   b. ripe   c. early-maturing   d. clever

4. superimpose   a. increase   b. lay over   c. improve   d. excel
5. prerequisite   a. requirement   b. reservation   c. influence   d. decision
6. semitone   a. soft sound   b. half note   c. shade of color   d. half step
7. transpose   a. send out   b. take place   c. overcome   d. switch

UNIT 56

A. Choose the closest definition:

1. multifarious   a. odd   b. varied   c. evil   d. unusual
2. multicellular   a. bacterial   b. viral   c. consisting of many cells   d. huge
3. multilateral
   a. many-eyed   b. many-armed   c. with many participants   d. many-angled
4. multidisciplinary
   a. punishment by several methods   b. involving several subject areas
   c. with many disciples   d. punishment by different people

B. Match the definition on the left to the correct word on the right:

1.	gap	a.	superlative
2.	ideal	b.	subpar
3.	equality	c.	lateral
4.	inferior	d.	nonpareil
5.	varied	e.	parity
6.	outstanding	f.	disparity
7.	equal-sided	g.	equilateral
8.	sidewise	h.	collateral
9.	incidental	i.	multifarious

C. Indicate whether the pairs have the same or different meanings:

1. equilibrium / weight   same ___ / different ___
2. collateral / many-sided   same ___ / different ___
3. subpar / below normal   same ___ / different ___
4. equable / steady   same ___ / different ___
5. lateral / backward   same ___ / different ___
6. adequacy / surplus   same ___ / different ___
7. equinox /May Day   same ___ / different ___
8. disparity / equality   same ___ / different ___
9. equilateral / equal-sided   same ___ / different ___
10. nonpareil / unlikely   same ___ / different ___
11. bilateral / two-sided   same ___ / different ___

12. equilibrium / imbalance   same ___ / different ___
13. parity / equality   same ___ / different ___

D. Fill in each blank with the correct letter:

a. equinox	e. multidisciplinary	i. adequacy
b. multicellular	f. equable	j. multilateral
c. equilibrium	g. disparity	k. semiconductor
d. nonpareil	h. multifarious	

1. They're a quiet, pleasant couple, with very ____ temperaments.
2. Each year there seemed to be a larger ____ between their expected income and what they actually earned.
3. The U.S. has been participating in ____ climate talks with the rest of the world's biggest polluters.
4. Daylight saving time begins in March, shortly before the ____ and the arrival of spring.
5. There was more than enough water, but he worried about the ____ of their food supplies.
6. Arriving at college from his little high school, he was delighted but overwhelmed by the ____ course choices that were open to him.
7. The subject of economics can often be approached in a ____ way, since it usually involves mathematics, sociology, political science, and other fields.
8. Thousands of microscopic transistors partly made of the same ____ are embedded in each chip.
9. The smallest ____ organisms actually seem to have at least 1,000 cells, while the human body has trillions.
10. She's a ____ classroom teacher—enthusiastic, knowledgeable, concerned, entertaining, funny, everything a teacher should be.
11. In a healthy economy, supply and demand are in a state of approximate ____.

E. Fill in each blank with the correct letter:

a. equilateral	e. disparity	i. bilateral
b. parity	f. collateral	j. nonpareil
c. lateral	g. precocious	
d. multidisciplinary	h. subpar	

1. Customers kept complaining that the quality of the product was ____, so we eventually stopped selling it completely.
2. The Defense Department is headquartered in a huge building that forms an ____ pentagon.
3. She was a smart and ____ child who could read by the age of three.
4. She's concerned about the ____ between the performance on standardized tests and what she sees when she sits in on actual classes.
5. The departure of the factory cost the community 150 jobs, and the ____ effects on the town's economy were severe.

6. For 25 years it has prided itself on being the ____ Japanese restaurant in the city.
7. The two countries have been holding ____ talks, but the other countries in the region will be joining the process soon.
8. Since the 1970s women have been demanding ____ in pay with men, but they still lag well behind.
9. His trainer is teaching him ____ weight lifts, in which you hold your arms out to the sides.
10. The journal is devoted to water, taking a ____ approach that involves chemistry, physics, biology, and environmental science.

UNIT 57

A. Choose the closest definition:
1. Stratosphere
   a. cloud level b. sea level c. atmospheric layer d. outer space

B. Match the definition on the left to the correct word on the right:
1.	telecommute	a.	layer
2.	spherical	b.	upper atmosphere
3.	telemetry	c.	work electronically from home
4.	hemisphere	d.	long-distance measurement
5.	stratum	e.	half-sphere
6.	telegenic	f.	well-suited to television
7.	biosphere	g.	globelike
8.	stratosphere	h.	relating to design or purpose
9.	teleological	i.	life zone

C. Indicate whether the pairs have the same or different meanings:
1. nanostructure / enclosed mall   same ___ / different ___
2. telemetry / space travel   same ___ / different ___
3. stratum / layer   same ___ / different ___
4. teleological / systematic   same ___ / different ___
5. substrate / topic   same ___ / different ___
6. nanotechnology / computer science   same ___ / different ___
7. stratification / strategy   same ___ / different ___
8. nanosecond / million seconds   same ___ / different ___
9. stratocumulus / puffy summer clouds   same ___ / different ___
10. nanoparticle / thousand particles   same ___ / different ___

D. Fill in each blank with the correct letter:

a. nanoparticle   e. telegenic   i. hemisphere
b. telecommute   f. spherical   j. nanosecond
c. substrate   g. nanostructure k. teleological
d. nanotechnology h. telemetry

1. Wildlife zoologists use ____ to track the migration habits of the caribou.
2. The philosopher's argument was ____ in that it looked for a design or purpose in natural phenomena.
3. A ____ is something whose size is measured in billionths of a meter.
4. Her boss has given her permission to ____ two days a week, using a computer hookup from home.
5. Each picture illustrates a different ____ (a nanotube, a nanorod, a nanowire, etc.), each of which has its own set of important uses.
6. He raced down the hall and was back in about a ____ with the good news.
7. The stone was roughly ____, but it didn't roll easily.
8. Some newscasters seem to have been hired for nothing more than their ____ smiles.
9. My trip to Australia was the first time I had left this ____.
10. Amateurs can often grow mushrooms successfully on a ____ of sawdust, hay, or even coffee grounds.
11. Many scientists believe that ____ is the most exciting field in the physical sciences today, with possible uses in almost every aspect of life.

E. Fill in each blank with the correct letter:

a. stratocumulus   e. biosphere   i. telepathic
b. hemisphere   f. nanotechnology j. substrate
c. telegenic   g. stratification k. spherical
d. stratum   h. stratosphere

1. Every living thing that we know of inhabits the earth's ____.
2. He was successful in radio but not ____ enough to succeed on television.
3. The ____ contains the ozone layer, which guards the earth against excessive ultraviolet radiation.
4. The coral may use any hard surface as its ____, so artificial reefs have been created by sinking old ships.
5. As soon as his normal baseball season is over, my nephew joins a team in the southern ____, where spring training is just starting.
6. In old mill towns you could actually see the social ____, since the wealthy people lived on the high ground and the working class lived down below.
7. The possible future medical uses of the tiny particles and structures employed in ____ seem to be limited only by scientists' imaginations.
8. Football and rugby balls are ovoid, unlike the ____ balls used in other sports.
9. It was a typical winter sky, covered in a gray layer of ____ clouds.
10. The experiment showed that her claim to have ____ powers was false.

11. The ____ under the topsoil consisted of yellow lime mixed with gravel, and the one below that was of slatelike rock.

UNIT 58

A. Match the definition on the left to the correct word on the right:

1.	ambivalent	a.	courage
2.	prevalent	b.	masculinity
3.	triumvirate	c.	confirm
4.	ambiguous	d.	strong woman
5.	virago	e.	skill
6.	validate	f.	widespread
7.	ambit	g.	three-person board
8.	virtuosity	h.	similar in value
9.	valor	i.	having more than one meaning
10.	virility	j.	wavering
11.	ambient	k.	range
12.	equivalent	l.	ending

B. Indicate whether the pairs have the same or different meanings:

1. polyp / oyster   same ___ / different ___
2. polymer / molecule with repeating units   same ___ / different ___
3. ambient / atmospheric   same ___ / different ___
4. polyglot / speaking many languages   same ___ / different ___
5. polygraph / lie detector   same ___ / different ___
6. ambiguous / unclear   same ___ / different ___
7. polyphonic / religious   same ___ / different ___
8. valor / bravery   same ___ / different ___
9. triumvirate / three-person group   same ___ / different ___

C. Complete the analogy:

1. rare : scarce :: prevalent : ____
   a. unique b. commonplace c. thick d. preferred
2. vamp : sexy :: virago : ____
   a. loud b. attractive c. powerful d. elderly
3. anxious : calm :: ambivalent : ____
   a. neutral b. certain c. funloving d. jittery
4. femininity : man :: virility : ____
   a. female b. girl c. woman d. lady

5. local : here :: ambient : ____
   a. there b. somewhere c. nowhere d. everywhere

D. Fill in each blank with the correct letter:

a. virago	e. valor	i. ambivalent
b. virtuosity	f. validate	j. polymer
c. triumvirate	g. prevalent	k. ambit
d. virility	h. equivalent	l. polyglot

1. Some people think a man's ____ fades with age.
2. An election worker at the next table will ____ each voter's ID.
3. The orchestra will be performing with a solo violinist whose ____ has already made her a star.
4. Colds and flu threaten to be unusually ____ this winter.
5. The development of the first synthetic ____ for use as fabric revolutionized the garment industry.
6. The ranch is owned by Mamie Peabody, a brawny ____ who sometimes competes in the men's events at the rodeo.
7. We may not be able to find an identical chair, but we'll find an ____ one.
8. A real ____, she could speak four languages and read three others.
9. He reminded the audience that particle physics didn't really fall within the ____ of his expertise.
10. The company is really run by a ____: Bailey, Sanchez, and Dr. Ross.
11. At a memorial ceremony, the slain guard who had tried to stop the gunman was honored for ____.
12. Jessica was ____ about going to the party: it sounded exciting, but she wouldn't know any of the other guests.

E. Fill in each blank with the correct letter:

a. polyglot	e. ambient	i. equivalent
b. ambiguous	f. virtuosity	j. polyp
c. validate	g. polymer	k. ambivalent
d. polygraph	h. ambit	

1. An endorsement from one of the major medical associations would help ____ the therapies we offer.
2. Rubber is a natural ____ that remains the preferred material for many uses.
3. She felt ____ about the invitation, and couldn't decide whether to accept or decline.
4. She had never passed a ____ test, since apparently her heart rate always shot up when she was asked a question.
5. A speed of 100 kilometers per hour is ____ to about 60 miles per hour.
6. Lord Raglan's ____ order confused the commander of the Light Brigade and led to its disastrous charge.
7. Having gone to school in four countries as a child, she was already a fluent ____.
8. The subject really falls within the ____ of economics rather than sociology.

9. She was renowned for her ___ in the kitchen, whipping up delicious meals from any ingredients that came to hand.
10. The medical tests had revealed a suspicious-looking ___ on his stomach.
11. When the ___ light is low, photographers use a flash.

UNIT 59

A. Choose the closest definition:

1. orthodox — a. straight b. pier c. conventional d. waterfowl
2. rectify — a. redo b. make right c. modify d. make longer
3. odometer — a. intelligence measurer b. heart-rate measurer c. height measurer d. mile measurer
4. orthopedics — a. foot surgery b. children's medicine c. medical dictionaries d. treatment of skeletal defects
5. directive — a. leader b. sign c. order d. straightener
6. metric — a. relating to poetic rhythm b. relating to ocean depth c. relating to books d. relating to particles of matter
7. orthography — a. correct color b. correct map c. correct direction d. correct spelling
8. rectitude — a. roughness b. integrity c. certainty d. sameness
9. tachometer — a. rpm measurer b. sharpness measurer c. fatigue measurer d. size measurer
10. orthodontics — a. dentistry for children b. dentistry for gums c. dentistry for crooked teeth d. dentistry for everyone
11. rectilinear — a. employing straight lines b. employing curved lines c. employing 45° angles d. employing circles
12. meter — a. weight b. rhythm c. speed d. force

B. Indicate whether the pairs have the same or different meanings:

1. rectify / damage — same ___ / different ___
2. orthodox / crucial — same ___ / different ___
3. rectitude / honesty — same ___ / different ___
4. orthopedics / broken bones — same ___ / different ___
5. rectilinear / straight — same ___ / different ___
6. directive / question — same ___ / different ___
7. orthography / architecture — same ___ / different ___
8. orthodontics / fixing of crooked teeth — same ___ / different ___
9. rectify / straighten — same ___ / different ___
10. orthopedics / shoe repair — same ___ / different ___
11. rectilinear / curvy — same ___ / different ___

12. orthodox / Christian   same ___ / different ___
13. rectitude / stubbornness   same ___ / different ___

C. Match the definition on the left to the correct word on the right:

1.	meter	a.	rotation meter
2.	tachometer	b.	distance measurer
3.	metric	c.	relating to a measuring system
4.	odometer	d.	beat pattern

D. Fill in each blank with the correct letter:

a. orthography   c. orthodontics   e. directive
b. tachometer   d. metric

1. Their department had received a ___ that morning regarding flexibility in the work schedule.
2. Every scientist in the world uses a version of the ___ system, but the American public has always resisted it.
3. He argues that ___ is more important than ever, since the success of your Web searches depends on your spelling.
4. After graduation from dental school, Kyle took a postgraduate course in ___.
5. When the traffic gets too noisy, I have to glance at the ___ to see if the engine is racing.

E. Complete the analogy:

1. radical : rebellious :: orthodox : ___
   a. routine   b. conventional   c. sane   d. typical
2. identify : name :: rectify : ___
   a. make over   b. make new   c. make right   d. make up

A. 1.c 2.b 3.d 4.d 5.c 6.a 7.d 8.b 9.a 10.c 11.a 12.b
B. 1.d 2.d 3.s 4.d 5.s 6.d 7.d 8.s 9.s 10.d 11.d 12.d 13.d
C. 1.d 2.a 3.c 4.b   D. 1.e 2.d 3.a 4.c 5.b   E. 1.b 2.c

UNIT 60

A. Choose the closest definition:

1.	Immutable	a. unalterable b. transformable c. inaudible d. audible
2.	travesty	a. farce b. outfit c. transportation d. success
3.	permutation	a. continuation b. splendor c. disorder d. rearrangement
4.	divest	a. add on b. take off c. take in d. add up
5.	choreography	a. book design b. dance script c. choir practice d. bird study

B. Match the definition on the left to the correct word on the right:

1.	installing in office	a.	transient
2.	cross-dresser	b.	travesty
3.	bad imitation	c.	lithograph
4.	print	d.	choreography
5.	get rid of	e.	divest
6.	dance design	f.	hagiography
7.	saint's biography	g.	calligraphy
8.	beautiful handwriting	h.	transvestite
9.	brief	i.	investiture

C. Indicate whether the pairs have the same or different meanings:

1. transmute / endanger   same ___ / different ___
2. transient / temporary   same ___ / different ___
3. transcendent / sublime   same ___ / different ___
4. transfiguration / transformation   same ___ / different ___
5. transponder / radio signaler same ___ / different ___
6. divest / get rid of   same ___ / different ___
7. transvestite / cross-dresser same ___ / different ___

D. Fill in each blank with the correct letter:

a. choreography   c. commute   e. investiture
b. lithograph   d. calligraphy   f. hagiography

1. The book was pure ___, painting its statesman hero as not only brilliant but saintly.
2. A signed ___ by Picasso wouldn't be valued nearly as highly as one of his paintings.
3. She admired the ___, but the dancers didn't seem to have practiced enough.
4. The ___ of the society's new leader was a secret and solemn event.
5. In his spare time he practiced ___, using special pens to write short quotations suitable for framing.
6. After having reviewed the new evidence that had come to light, the governor decided to ___ the sentence.

E. Complete the analogy:

1. hostile : friendly :: immutable : ___
   a. changeable b. decaying c. breathable d. out of date
2. permit : allow :: commute : ___
   a. review b. claim c. substitute d. send
3. order : sequence :: permutation : ___
   a. addition b. notion c. rearrangement d. removal
4. transmit : send :: transmute : ___
   a. transit b. transform c. transfer d. transport

F. Choose the closest definition:

1. immutable   a. unchangeable   b. immature   c. noisy   d. defiant
2. permutation   a. evolution   b. rearrangement   c. approval   d. inflation
3. commute   a. deposit   b. invest   c. discuss   d. change
4. transmute   a. reconsider   b. send away   c. silence   d. convert

G. Fill in each blank with the correct letter:

a. transcendent   d. travesty   g. transfiguration
b. transvestite   e. transponder   h. divest
c. transient   f. investiture

1. The ___ of the prime minister was an occasion of pomp and ceremony.
2. Since all the judges were cronies of the dictator, the court proceedings were a ___ of justice.
3. The young model became a notorious success when she was discovered to be a ___.
4. The community is surrounded by a high wall, and the gate opens only when signaled by a resident's ___.
5. The new director planned to ___ the museum of two of its Picassos.
6. On the rare occasions when he conducts nowadays, the critics rave about his ___ performances of the great Mahler symphonies.
7. Painters have tried to depict Jesus' ___ on the mountaintop, while realizing that it's probably impossible to do with mere paint.
8. Painters are well aware of how ___ the color effects of the sunset are, and how the sky often looks completely different after five minutes.

UNIT 61

A. Choose the closest definition:

1. iconoclast   a. icon painter   b. dictator   c. dissident   d. tycoon
2. comprehend   a. misjudge   b. confirm   c. grasp   d. gather
3. iconic   a. wealthy   b. famous   c. indirect   d. symbolic
4. reprehensible
   a. understandable   b. reptilian   c. disgraceful   d. approachable
5. icon   a. psychic   b. leader   c. symbol   d. prophet

B. Indicate whether the pairs have the same or different meanings:

1. prehensile / dropping   same ___ / different ___
2. reprehensible / unusual   same ___ / different ___
3. comprehend / include   same ___ / different ___

4. apprehend / arrest   same ___ / different ___
5. sensitive / susceptible   same ___ / different ___
6. noticeable / perceptible   same ___ / different ___
7. iconic / symbolic   same ___ / different ___

C. Fill in each blank with the correct letter:

a. iconic	f. intercept	k. pervade
b. persevere	g. iconoclast	l. perceptible
c. susceptible	h. percolate	m. prehensile
d. iconography	i. reception	
e. permeate	j. icon	

1. Before the Internet, it took many years before these ideas began to ____ the barriers that the government had set up.
2. He enjoyed being an ___, since he had a lot of odd ideas and arguing suited his personality well.
3. We know that drugs now ____ the blue-collar workplace in many small Midwestern towns.
4. Thirty years later, his great speech was viewed as an ___ moment in modern American history.
5. The hands of even a newborn infant are ____ and surprisingly strong.
6. By the fall there had been a ____ change in the mood of the students.
7. The strange ____ of the painting had caught her attention years ago, and she continued to puzzle over the obviously symbolic appearance of various odd objects.
8. They had come back from Russia with a beautiful ____ of Mary and another of St. Basil.
9. The liquid began to ____ through the blend of herbs and spices, giving off a delicious scent.
10. They waited weeks to hear about the board's ____ of their proposal.
11. She's extremely stubborn, so I'm sure she's going to ___ until the whole thing is completed.
12. Small children are often ____ to nightmares after hearing ghost stories in the dark.
13. He was at the post office the next morning, hoping to ____ the foolish letter he had sent yesterday.

D. Complete the analogy:

1. allow : permit :: apprehend : ____
   a. accept b. ignore c. figure out d. examine
2. permit : allow :: permeate : ____
   a. ignore b. move c. penetrate d. recover

E. Choose the closest definition:

1. apprehend   a. seize b. insist c. understand d. deny
2. intercept   a. throw b. seize c. arrest d. close
3. persevere   a. carry off b. resume c. inquire d. carry on

4. reprehensible   a. understandable b. worthy of blame
                    c. worthy of return d. inclusive
5. perceptible   a. noticeable b. capable c. readable d. thinkable
6. percolate   a. boil b. spread c. restore d. seep
7. comprehend   a. take b. understand c. compress d. remove
8. prehensile
    a. able to peel b. able to swing c. able to howl d. able to grasp

F. Match the definition on the left to the correct word on the right:

1.	susceptible	a.	seep
2.	icon	b.	symbol
3.	persevere	c.	spread into
4.	reception	d.	keep going
5.	iconoclast	e.	artistic symbolism
6.	pervade	f.	symbolic
7.	perceptible	g.	dissenter
8.	iconography	h.	fill with something
9.	permeate	i.	noticeable
10.	intercept	j.	seize
11.	iconic	k.	easily influenced
12.	percolate	l.	receiving

UNIT 62

A. Complete the analogy:

1. grab : seize :: cede : ____   a. hang on b. hand over c. hang up d. head out
2. disagree : argue :: concede : ____   a. drive b. hover c. yield d. refuse
3. swerve : veer :: accede : ____   a. agree b. descent c. reject d. demand
4. etiquette : manners :: precedent : ____
    a. courtesy b. tradition c. rudeness d. behavior
5. better : inferior :: anterior : ____   a. before b. beside c. above d. behind
6. allow : forbid :: cede : ____   a. take b. agree c. soothe d. permit
7. complain : whine :: accede : ____
    a. go over b. give in c. give out d. go along

B. Indicate whether the pairs have the same or different meanings:

1.	interpolate / fill up	same ___ / different ___
2.	antedate / occur before	same ___ / different ___
3.	intercede / invade	same ___ / different ___

4. cede / acquire same ___ / different ___
5. retrogress / go backward same ___ / different ___

C. Fill in each blank with the correct letter:

a. antedate	e. retrofit	i. interdict
b. retrospective	f. accede	j. antechamber
c. pervade	g. antecedent	k. retrogress
d. anterior	h. retroactive	

1. She turns 70 this year, and the museum is honoring her with a huge ___.
2. Please step into the judge's ___; she'll be with you in a few minutes.
3. The navy plans to ___ a fleet of 25-year-old ships to increase their speed and monitoring capacity.
4. More agents will be needed to ___ the drugs being carried north to Panama from Colombia.
5. In *Lord of the Flies*, a group of English schoolboys manages to ___ to a barely civilized state within a few months.
6. Some of the faculty have decided to quietly ___ to the students' request for less homework.
7. Although the tax increase wasn't passed until June, its effect was ___ to the first of the year.
8. The British would say "The company are proud of their record," since they treat "the company" as a plural ___.
9. She was tempted to ___ the letter to make it seem that she had not forgotten to write it but only to mail it.
10. A butterfly's antennae are located on the most ___ part of its body.
11. He senses that a negative tone has begun to ___ the school in the last couple of years.

D. Match the definition on the left to the correct word on the right:

1.	retrogress	b.	effective as of earlier
2.	antechamber	c.	block
3.	interdict	d.	what comes before
4.	retrospective	e.	chink
5.	antedate	f.	review of a body of work
6.	interpolate	g.	revert to an earlier state
7.	retrofit	h.	ask for mercy
8.	anterior	i.	modernize
9.	intercede	j.	waiting room
10.	retroactive	k.	toward the front
11.	antecedent	l.	to date before
12.	interstice	m.	stick in

E. Choose the closest definition:

1. interdict   a. scold b. allow c. cut off d. intrude
2. retrofit   a. insert b. dress up c. update d. move back

3. interstice   a. filling   b. gap   c. layer   d. village
4. retrospective   a. backward glance   b. exhibit of an artist's work
                 c. illusion of depth   d. difference of opinion

F. Fill in each blank with the correct letter:

a. interdict	e. concede	i. retrofit
b. precedent	f. antechamber	j. interpolate
c. retroactive	g. intercede	k. cede
d. interstice	h. accede	

1. The door to the ruined barn was locked, but through an ____ in the wall I glimpsed an old tractor and several odd pieces of machinery.
2. They were shown into an elegant ____ where they awaited their audience with the king.
3. It cost millions to ____ each fighter jet with new navigational instruments.
4. She would go on talking about her country by the hour, while I would occasionally ____ a comment to show that I was paying attention.
5. She's very stubborn, and in an argument she'll never ____ a single point.
6. The country's small coast guard hopes to ____ most of the arms at sea before they can reach the guerrilla fighters.
7. Only after I got the coach to ____ did the principal agree to change my suspension to probation.
8. The treaty requires that both sides ____ several small tracts of land.
9. After lengthy negotiations, the union will probably ____ to several of the company's terms.
10. Since his salary review was delayed by a few weeks, his boss made the raise ____ to the beginning of the month.
11. The judges could find no ____ to guide them in deciding how to deal with the case.

UNIT 63

A. Choose the closest definition:

1. microbe   a. miniature ball   b. tiny organism   c. infection   d. midget
2. temperance   a. wrath   b. modesty   c. moderation   d. character
3. microclimate
    a. short period of different weather   b. weather in Micronesia
    c. weather at the microscopic level   d. special climate of a small area
4. distemper   a. anger   b. hysteria   c. disease   d. weakness
5. microbrew   a. small serving of beer   b. half-cup of coffee
                 c. beer from a small brewery   d. tea in a small container

6. symbiosis   a. musical instrument b. independence
                  c. community d. interdependence
7. microbiologist   a. one who studies small insects b. small scientist
                  c. one who grows small plants d. one who studies bacteria and viruses

B. Fill in each blank with the correct letter:

a. kleptomania	e. microbe	i. temper
b. microbrew	f. biodegradable	j. megalomaniac
c. biopsy	g. dipsomaniac	k. microclimate
d. egomaniac	h. microbiologist	

1. Their bags are made of ____ plastic that they claim will break down within two months.
2. Researchers are interested in the role played in the disease by a ____ that no one had particularly noticed before.
3. By now the dictator had begun to strike some observers as a possibly dangerous ____.
4. For a young ____ like herself, it seemed that the most interesting job possibilities lay in the study of viruses.
5. After finding several of her missing things in the other closet, she began wondering if her roommate was an ordinary thief or actually suffering from ____.
6. Their 25-acre property, a bowl-shaped field surrounded by woods, had its own ____ which was perfect for certain fruit trees.
7. A medical report from 1910 had identified her great-grandfather as a ____, and ten years later his alcoholism would kill him.
8. Doctors recommended a ____ in case the X-ray had missed something.
9. At the state fair their beer was judged Minnesota's best ____.
10. Many of us take milk or cream with our coffee to ____ its acidity.
11. Her boss was an ____ who always needed someone around telling him how brilliant he was.

C. Match the definition on the left to the correct word on the right:

1. distemper   a. animal disease
2. egomaniac   b. alcoholic
3. temperance   c. moderation
4. dipsomaniac   d. person deluded by thoughts of grandeur
5. temper   e. mix or moderate
6. megalomaniac   f. compulsive thieving
7. intemperate   g. unrestrained
8. kleptomania   h. extremely self-centered person

D. Indicate whether the pairs have the same or different meanings:

1. bionic / fantastic   same ___ / different ___
2. biopsy / life story   same ___ / different ___
3. symbiosis / shared existence   same ___ / different ___

4. biodegradable / readily broken down   same ___ / different ___
5. bionic / artificial   same ___ / different ___

E. Complete the analogy:

1. enthusiastic : eager :: intemperate : ___
    a. calm b. amused c. restrained d. uncontrolled

F. Fill in each blank with the correct letter:

a. intemperate	d. biodegradable	g. bionic
b. symbiosis	e. microclimate	h. distemper
c. temperance	f. temper	i. biopsy

1. By their careful planting on this south-facing hillside, they had created a ___ that was perfect for certain crops that no one else was able to grow.
2. Scientists are working on new ___ devices to enable amputees to do detailed manual work.
3. Don thinks we had better ___ our enthusiasm for this scheme with a large dose of skepticism.
4. Just about everything in our bodies is ___ except the fillings in our teeth.
5. She had a physical last week, and the doctor ordered a ___ of a suspicious looking patch of skin.
6. After 50 years of marriage, the ___ between them is just about total.
7. The widow leaped to her feet and launched into a shockingly ___ tirade at the jury.
8. That year, the local raccoon population had been severely reduced by an epidemic of ___.
9. Her eternal watchword was ___, and no one ever saw her upset, worn out, angry, or tipsy.

UNIT 64

A. Fill in each blank with the correct letter:

a. cadence	d. context	g. hypertext
b. textual	e. signify	h. decadent
c. cadenza	f. cadaver	i. subtext

1. When the sentence was taken out of ___, it sounded quite different.
2. The deeper meaning of many literary works lies in their ___.
3. Many young people wonder how anyone ever did research without the benefit of ___ links.

4. The soloist's ___ was breathtaking, and the audience burst into applause as he played his final notes.
5. Every time it seemed as if the piece was reaching its final ___, the harmony would shift and the music would continue.
6. In these auctions, bidders ___ that they're raising their bids by holding up a paddle with a number on it.
7. In those days grave robbers would dig up a ___ at night after the burial and deliver it to the medical school.
8. The study of poetry normally requires careful ___ analysis.
9. Her roommate's family struck her as ___, with the younger generation spending its huge allowances on expensive and unhealthy pleasures.

B. Choose the closest definition:

1. signet   a. stamp b. gold ring c. Pope's sign d. baby swan
2. insignia   a. indication b. signal c. badge d. rank
3. signify   a. sense b. remind c. sign d. mean
4. signatory   a. document b. agreement c. banner d. cosigner
5. textual a. of an idea b. of a manuscript c. on an assumption d. on a hunch
6. cadaver   a. patient b. skeleton c. zombie d. corpse

C. Fill in each blank with the correct letter:

a. context	d. necropsy	g. decadent
b. necrosis	e. subtext	h. necropolis
c. cadence	f. necromancer	

1. The frostbite was bad and there was a chance of ___ setting in, so we had to work fast.
2. The scene in the hip downtown nightclubs just seemed ___ and unhealthy to her.
3. Grief-stricken parents would go to the village ___, who would try to contact their dead children.
4. They were certain the cat hadn't died of natural causes, and the ___ revealed that they were right.
5. The men's graves in this Iron Age ___ held numerous weapons.
6. A piece of music that doesn't end with a firm ___ leaves most audiences tense and unsatisfied.
7. By taking his remarks out of ___, the papers made him look like a crook.
8. She claims that the novel has a ___ that no one has ever noticed, and pointed out the clues that the author had provided.

D. Indicate whether the pairs have the same or different meanings:

1. necropsy / autopsy   same ___ / different ___
2. cadenza / solo section   same ___ / different ___
3. necromancer / gravedigger   same ___ / different ___
4. cadaver / bodily organ   same ___ / different ___
5. necrosis / tissue death   same ___ / different ___
6. cadence / musical ending   same ___ / different ___

7.	necropolis / cemetery	same ___ / different ___
8.	decadent / morally declining	same ___ / different ___
9.	cadenza / side table	same ___ / different ___
10.	necropolis / graveyard	same ___ / different ___
11.	necrosis / black magic	same ___ / different ___
12.	signer / signatory	same ___ / different ___
13.	seal / signet	same ___ / different ___

E. Match the definition on the left to the correct word on the right:

1.	insignia	a.	relating to written matter
2.	hypertext	b.	underlying meaning
3.	signatory	c.	emblem of honor
4.	subtext	d.	engraved seal
5.	signet	e.	setting of spoken or written words
6.	textual	f.	signer
7.	signify	g.	computer links
8.	context	h.	indicate

A. 1.d 2.i 3.g 4.c 5.a 6.e 7.f 8.b 9.h B. 1.a 2.c 3.d 4.d 5.b 6.d
C. 1.b 2.g 3.f 4.i 5.h 6.c 7.a 8.e D. 1.c 2.e 3.d 4.d 5.a 6.a 7.a 8.e 9.d 10.a
11.d 12.a 13.a E. 1.c 2.g 3.f 4.b 5.d 6.a 7.h 8.e

UNIT 65

A. Choose the closest definition:

1.	atrophy	a. expansion b. swelling c. exercise d. wasting
2.	ectopic	a. amazing b. current c. reserved d. out of place
3.	hypertrophy	a. excessive growth b. low birth rate
		c. increased speed d. inadequate nutrition
4.	dystrophy	a. bone development b. muscular wasting
		c. nerve growth d. muscle therapy
5.	eutrophication	a. inadequate moisture b. excessive growth
		c. loss of sunlight d. healthy nourishment

B. Fill in each blank with the correct letter:

a. ectopic	e. psyche	i. atrophy
b. psychedelic	f. eutrophication	j. topography
c. hypertrophy	g. topical	k. psychosomatic
d. utopian	h. psychotherapist	l. dystrophy

1. They'd only been together two weeks, but already she suspected there was a lot hidden in the depths of her boyfriend's ___.
2. The ___ of a river valley often includes a wide, fertile floodplain.
3. In muscular ___, the wasting begins in the legs and advances to the arms.

4. His fear of AIDs was so intense that he'd been developing ___ symptoms, which his doctor hardly bothered to check out anymore.
5. Since he hates needles, he asks his dentist to use only a ___ anesthetic inside his mouth.
6. He hated the thought of drugs but knew he needed someone to talk to, so his brother recommended a local ___.
7. By then the pond had almost entirely filled in with plant life, a result of the ___ caused by the factory's discharges.
8. In the four weeks before he has the cast taken off, his muscles will ___ quite a lot.
9. Testing ___ drugs on cancer patients was difficult because of their unpredictable mental effects.
10. An ___ pregnancy is an unusual event that poses serious medical problems.
11. In 1970 they founded a ___ community on a 400-acre farm, where all property was to be owned in common.
12. Muscular ___ as extreme as that is only possible with steroids.

C. Match the definition on the left to the correct word on the right:

1.	psyche	a.	entropy
2.	topical	b.	mind
3.	decay	c.	heliotrope
4.	psychotherapist	d.	caused by the mind
5.	utopian	e.	tropism
6.	fragrant flower	f.	producing hallucinations
7.	psychosomatic	g.	psychotropic
8.	ectopic	h.	landscape features
9.	automatic motion	i.	"talk" doctor
10.	psychedelic	j.	away from its usual place
11.	topography	k.	of current interest
12.	affecting the mind	l.	ideal

D. Indicate whether the pairs have the same or different meanings:

1.	tropism / growth	same ___ / different ___
2.	atrophy / enlarge	same ___ / different ___
3.	entropy / disorder	same ___ / different ___
4.	hypertrophy / overgrowth	same ___ / different ___
5.	heliotrope / sunflower	same ___ / different ___
6.	psychotropic / mind-altering	same ___ / different ___
7.	topography / land's features	same ___ / different ___
8.	soul / psyche	same ___ / different ___

UNIT 66

A. Choose the closest definition:

1. hypothermia   a. excitability   b. subnormal temperature
   c. external temperature   d. warmth
2. ideology   a. notion   b. philosophy   c. standard   d. concept
3. hypoglycemia   a. extreme heat   b. low blood sugar
   c. low energy   d. high blood pressure
4. methodology   a. endurance   b. patience   c. authority   d. system
5. cardiology   a. ear specialty   b. heart specialty
   c. brain specialty   d. nerve specialty
6. hypertension   a. anxiety   b. tightness
   c. high blood pressure   d. duodenal ulcer
7. hypothetical   a. typical   b. substandard   c. sympathetic   d. assumed
8. physiology   a. sports medicine   b. body language
   c. study of medicine   d. study of organisms
9. hypochondriac
   a. person with imaginary visions   b. person with heart congestion
   c. person with imaginary ailments   d. person with imaginary relatives

B. Indicate whether the pairs have the same or different meanings:

1. hypochondriac / wise man   same ___ / different ___
2. cardiology / game theory   same ___ / different ___
3. hypoglycemia / high blood sugar   same ___ / different ___
4. epidermis / outer skin   same ___ / different ___
5. ideology / beliefs   same ___ / different ___
6. hypothetical / supposed   same ___ / different ___
7. physiology / bodybuilding   same ___ / different ___
8. hypothermia / low blood sugar   same ___ / different ___
9. methodology / carefulness   same ___ / different ___
10. dermal / skin-related   same ___ / different ___
11. hypothermia / heatstroke   same ___ / different ___
12. physiology / sports medicine   same ___ / different ___

C. Match the definition on the left to the correct word on the right:

1. hyperactive   a.   breathe deeply and rapidly
2. dermatitis   b.   overly active
3. hyperventilate   c.   extreme overstatement
4. hypertension   d.   skin rash
5. methodology   e.   high blood pressure
6. hyperbole   f.   procedure

D. Complete the analogy:

1. brief : extended :: hyperactive : ___
   a. exaggerated   b. young   c. required   d. calm

2. awareness : ignorance :: hyperbole : ___
   a. exaggeration b. understatement c. calm d. excitement

E. Fill in each blank with the correct letter:

a. taxidermist	e. hypertension	i. atrophy
b. hyperactive	f. topiary	j. epidermis
c. topical	g. dermal	k. hyperventilate
d. dermatitis	h. hyperbole	l. hypochondriac

1. After spending four years at home, she's afraid her professional skills have begun to ___.
2. To get rid of wrinkles, you can have a ___ filler injected into parts of your face.
3. He had a mild form of ___ that occasionally produced a rash on his upper arms.
4. In yoga class we're often warned not to ___ during our breathing exercises.
5. The ___ keeps the body waterproof and provides a barrier against infection.
6. Before beginning to drill, the dentist applies a ___ anesthetic.
7. They had come across a dead eagle in perfect condition, and a ___ had done a beautiful job of mounting it for display.
8. A ___ imagination can transform every creak and rustle in a dark house into a threat.
9. In her middle age she became a thorough ___, always convinced she was suffering from some new disease.
10. The city maintains a small ___ garden full of trees and bushes in all sorts of shapes.
11. She's warned me that there's plenty of ___ in her brother's big talk and that I shouldn't take it too seriously.
12. Both my parents are on medication for ___, and the doctor monitors their blood pressure regularly.

F. Choose the word that does not belong:

1. ideology   a. essay b. philosophy c. principles d. beliefs

UNIT 67

A. Choose the closest definition:

1. dynamo   a. powerhouse b. force unit
                   c. time interval d. power outage

2. aerodynamic   a. glamorously smooth b. relating to movement through air
                 c. using oxygen for power d. atmospherically charged
3. dynamic   a. explosive b. energetic c. excited d. dangerous
4. hydrodynamic a. relating to moving fluids b. water-resistant
                 c. relating to boats d. relating to water

B. Indicate whether the pairs have the same or different meanings:

1. hematology / liver medicine   same ___ / different ___
2. podiatrist / children's doctor   same ___ / different ___
3. aerodynamic / air-powered   same ___ / different ___
4. hemorrhage / blood circulation   same ___ / different ___
5. dynamo / generator   same ___ / different ___
6. geriatric / bacterial   same ___ / different ___
7. hydrodynamic / tidal   same ___ / different ___
8. dynamic / electric   same ___ / different ___

C. Fill in each blank with the correct letter:

a. hepatitis	d. hemophilia	g. hemoglobin
b. hematology	e. bursitis	h. tendinitis
c. bronchitis	f. hemorrhage	

1. After a week of lifting boxes he got a case of ___, and they had to get movers in to finish the packing.
2. Blood samples get sent to the ___ department for analysis.
3. From the yellowness of her eyes, he suspected that it was a serious case of ___.
4. Soon after they start playing tennis and golf each spring, they both find they've developed ___ and have to give it up for a while.
5. He's a heavy smoker, and for several years he's been suffering from ___ several times a year.
6. Oxygen turns the ___ in the blood bright red; when the oxygen is removed, it becomes bluish.
7. The bleeding caused by the accident all seemed to be close to the surface, and there was no evidence of an internal ___.
8. The family had a history of ___, so she was naturally worried when her 3-year-old's wound kept bleeding for an hour.

D. Match the definition on the left to the correct word on the right:

1. lung inflammation   a.   bronchitis
2. liver disease   b.   iatrogenic
3. doctor-caused   c.   hepatitis

E. Fill in each blank with the correct letter:

a. bariatric	d. bariatric	g. dermal
b. iatrogenic	e. geriatric	h. geriatric
c. dynamic	f. podiatrist	i. hyperventilate

1. Following his ___ surgery his weight dropped from 310 pounds to 220.
2. Because of the doctor's bad handwriting, the pharmacist had given her the wrong medicine, and she had sued, claiming her new condition was ___ in origin.
3. ___ patients receive most of the country's medical care every year.
4. When my 12-year-old gets anxious, he often starts to ___, and it's caused him to pass out a couple of times.
5. After her last Kung Fu class she had a badly swollen foot, and her ___ was having some X-rays taken.
6. In the past she's gotten ___ silicone injections to erase her facial wrinkles.
7. With the growing elderly population, there's a crying need for more ___ specialists.
8. By all accounts, he was a ___ and forceful individual.
9. After years of failure at reducing, she was finally told by her doctor that ___ surgery was probably her best hope.

A. 1. 2. 3. 4. B. 1. 2. 3. 4. 5. 6. 7. 8.
C. 1. 2. 3. 4. 5. 6. 7. 8. D. 1. 2. 3.
E. 1. 2. 3. 4. 5. 6. 7. 8. 9.

UNIT 68

A. Choose the closest definition:

1. cantata   a. snack bar   b. pasta dish   c. sung composition   d. farewell gesture
2. incantation   a. ritual chant   b. ceremony   c. solemn march   d. recorded song
3. descant   a. climb downward   b. added melody
               c. supposed inability   d. writing table
4. cantor   a. singer   b. refusal   c. traitor   d. gallop
5. dynamo   a. explosive   b. missile   c. generator   d. electric weapon

B. Match the definition on the left to the correct word on the right:

1.	inaudible	a.	declare
2.	ultrasonic	b.	impossible to hear
3.	declaim	c.	noisy din
4.	auditory	d.	a critical hearing
5.	resonance	e.	speak formally
6.	acclamation	f.	unharmonious
7.	auditor	g.	financial examiner
8.	sonic	h.	acceptance with cheers
9.	proclaim	i.	continuing or echoing sound
10.	audition	j.	involving sound
11.	dissonant	k.	. beyond the hearing range
12.	clamor	l.	relating to hearing

C. Indicate whether the pairs have the same or different meanings:

1. dissonant / jarring   same ___ / different ___
2. incantation / chant   same ___ / different ___
3. inaudible / invisible   same ___ / different ___
4. cantor / conductor   same ___ / different ___
5. resonance / richness   same ___ / different ___
6. cantata / sonata   same ___ / different ___
7. audition / tryout   same ___ / different ___
8. descant / enchant   same ___ / different ___
9. ultrasonic / radical   same ___ / different ___
10. incantation / sacred dance   same ___ / different ___
11. auditor / performer   same ___ / different ___
12. sonic / loud   same ___ / different ___
13. auditory / hearing-related   same ___ / different ___

D. Match each word on the left to its *antonym* on the right:

1. inaudible   a.   harmonious
2. dissonant   b.   hearable

E. Fill in each blank with the correct letter:

a. auditor	d. clamor	g. cantor
b. declaim	e. cantata	h. acclamation
c. descant	f. proclaim	

1. As part of their musical training, she always encouraged them to sing their own ___ over the main melody.
2. The assembly approved the proposal by enthusiastic ___.
3. The university chorus was going to perform a Bach ___ along with the Mozart *Requiem*.
4. I got tired of hearing him ___ about how much better things were when he was young.
5. He began his singing career as a ___ in Brooklyn and ended it as an international opera star.
6. The networks could ___ the winner of the election as early as 7:00 p.m.
7. An ___ had been going over the company's financial records all week.
8. The proposed new tax was met with a ___ of protest.

F. Complete the analogy:

1. shout : whisper :: clamor : ___   a. noise   b. din   c. murmur   d. confusion
2. noisy : raucous :: dissonant : ___
    a. musical   b. symphonic   c. harsh   d. loud

UNIT 69

A. Choose the closest definition:

1. cataclysm   a. loud applause b. feline behavior c. disaster d. inspiration
2. thermal   a. boiling b. heat-related c. scorching d. cooked
3. catalyst   a. literary agent b. insurance agent
    c. cleaning agent d. agent of change
4. British thermal unit a. unit of electricity b. heat unit
    c. ocean current unit d. altitude unit
5. Catatonic   a. refreshing b. slow c. motionless d. boring
6. thermodynamics   a. science of motion b. nuclear science
    c. science of explosives d. science of heat energy
7. catacomb   a. underground road b. underground cemetery
    c. underground spring d. underground treasure
8. thermonuclear   a. nuclear reaction requiring high heat
    b. chemical reaction requiring a vacuum
    c. biological reaction producing bright light
    d. nuclear reaction based on distance from the sun

B. Match the definition on the left to the correct word on the right:

1. euphoria   a.   polite term
2. eulogy   b.   promoting superior offspring
3. eugenic   c.   great happiness
4. euphemism   d.   speech of praise

C. Fill in each blank with the correct letter:

    a. euphemism   d. acclamation   g. eugenic
    b. thermonuclear   e. euphoria   h. carcinogenic
    c. eulogy   f. declaim

1. She stood before the crowd and began to ____ in the tones of a practiced politician.
2. Huge cheering crowds in the streets greeted him on his return from exile, and he was swept into office almost by ____.
3. Her ____ for her longtime friend was the most moving part of the ceremony.
4. Since tobacco is well known to be a ____ substance, it's surprising that smoking is still legal.
5. The end of the war was marked by widespread ____ and celebration.
6. Though the dog is the product of generations of ____ breeding, she is high-strung and has terrible eyesight.
7. There is many a ____ for the word *die,* and many more for the word *drunk.*
8. Much thought has gone into the designing of ____ power plants that run on nuclear fusion.

D. Complete the analogy:

1. floral : flowers :: thermal : ____   a. weight   b. pressure   c. terms   d. heat
2. slang : vulgar :: euphemism : ____   a. habitual   b. polite   c. dirty   d. dumb
3. lively : sluggish :: catatonic : ____   a. active   b. petrified   c. feline   d. tired

E. Indicate whether the pairs have the same or different meanings:

1. cataclysm / disaster   same ___ / different ___
2. British thermal unit / calorie   same ___ / different ___
3. genesis / birth   same ___ / different ___
4. thermal / insulating   same ___ / different ___
5. catalyst / cemetery   same ___ / different ___
6. generator / electricity-producing machine   same ___ / different ___
7. thermonuclear / destructive   same ___ / different ___
8. catatonic / paralyzed   same ___ / different ___
9. carcinogenic / cancer-causing   same ___ / different ___
10. thermodynamics / explosives   same ___ / different ___
11. catacomb / catastrophe   same ___ / different ___
12. genre / animal group   same ___ / different ___
13. cataclysm / religious teachings   same ___ / different ___
14. thermal / soil-related   same ___ / different ___
15. catalyst / distributor   same ___ / different ___

F. Fill in each blank with the correct letter:

a. genre   d. genesis   g. eugenic
b. catacomb   e. euphoria
c. carcinogenic   f. generator

1. The ____ of the idea for his first novel lay in a casual remark by a stranger one afternoon in the park.
2. ____ experimentation has produced a new breed of sheep with thick, fast-growing wool.
3. Any insecticides that are known to be ____ have supposedly been banned by the federal government.
4. When they went to Rome, they made sure to visit at least one underground ____.
5. She loved various kinds of classical music, but the string quartet was one ____ that she could never warm up to.
6. About once a year, an ice storm knocks out the electricity, and we haul out the ____ to get everything going again.
7. They felt such ____ that they almost wept with joy.

UNIT 70

A. Choose the closest definition:

1. confluence   a. support   b. joining   c. certainty   d. outflow
2. punctual   a. deflated   b. cranky   c. prompt   d. careful
3. mellifluous   a. flowing slowly   b. flowing outward
        c. flowing smoothly   d. flowing downward
4. acupuncture   a. massage technique   b. arrow hole
        c. pinprick   d. needle therapy
5. effluent   a. wastewater   b. wealth   c. trash   d. sewer
6. punctilious   a. pointed   b. careful   c. prompt   d. unusual
7. affluence   a. suburb   b. excess   c. wealth   d. mall
8. compunction   a. desire   b. bravery   c. qualm   d. conviction

B. Match the definition on the left to the correct word on the right:

1. cosmopolitan   a.   small world
2. microcosm   b.   universe
3. cosmology   c.   description of the universe
4. cosmos   d.   well-traveled

C. Complete the analogy:

1. stable : constant :: erratic : ____
   a. fast   b. invisible   c. mistaken   d. unpredictable
2. split : separation :: confluence : ____
   a. breakup   b. division   c. flow   d. merging
3. descending : ascending :: errant : ____
   a. moving   b. wandering   c. fixed   d. straying
4. village : city :: microcosm : ____
   a. flea circus   b. universe   c. scale model   d. bacteria
5. fruitful : barren :: erroneous : ____
   a. productive   b. pleasant   c. targeted   d. correct
6. geology : earth :: cosmology : ____
   a. sophistication   b. universe   c. explanation   d. appearance
7. forest : trees :: cosmos : ____
   a. stars   b. earth   c. orbits   d. universe
8. typical : normal :: aberrant : ____
   a. burdened   b. roving   c. odd   d. missing
9. bold : shy :: cosmopolitan : ____
   a. planetary   b. naive   c. unique   d. nearby
10. lively : energetic :: erratic : ____
    a. calm   b. changeable   c. steady   d. weary

D. Indicate whether the pairs have the same or different meanings:

1. mellifluous / smooth   same ____ / different ____
2. punctilious / speedy   same ____ / different ____

3. effluent / pollutant   same ___ / different ___
4. acupuncture / precision   same ___ / different ___
5. confluence / understanding   same ___ / different ___
6. punctual / on time   same ___ / different ___
7. affluence / wealth   same ___ / different ___
8. compunction / threat   same ___ / different ___

E. Choose the closest definition:

1. compunction   a. confidence b. misgiving c. condition d. surprise
2. cosmopolitan   a. bored b. intelligent c. inexperienced d. well-traveled
3. effluent   a. discharge b. effort c. excess d. wealth
4. cosmos   a. chaos b. order c. universe d. beauty

F. Match each word on the left to its *antonym* on the right:

1. erroneous   a. true
2. aberrant   b. typical

G. Fill in each blank with the correct letter:

a. aberrant	d. affluence	g. erroneous
b. punctilious	e. erratic	
c. errant	f. mellifluous	

1. Her low opinion of him turned out to be based on several ___ assumptions.
2. She was so ___ about the smallest office policies that everyone went to her when they had forgotten one of them.
3. Like many malaria sufferers, she experienced ___ changes in her temperature.
4. Occasionally an ___ cow would be found on the back lawn, happily grazing on the fresh clover.
5. After several incidents of disturbingly ___ behavior, his parents began taking him to a psychiatrist.
6. Imperial Rome was a city of great ___ as well as terrible poverty.
7. The ___ tones of a Mozart flute concerto poured from the window.

A. 1.b 2.c 3.c 4.d 5.a 6.b 7.c 8.c B. 1.d 2.a 3.c 4.b C. 1.d 2.d 3.c 4.b 5.d
6.b 7.a 8.c 9.b 10.b D. 1.s 2.d 3.s 4.d 5.d 6.s 7.s 8.d E. 1.b 2.d 3.a 4.c
F. 1.a 2.b G. 1.g 2.b 3.e 4.c 5.a 6.d 7.f

UNIT 71

A. Choose the closest definition:

1. kinesiology   a. science of planetary motion b. atomic motion
                  c. study of human movement d. history of film

2. anthropoid a. tapirs and antelopes b. cats and dogs
   c. chimpanzees and gorillas d. salamanders and chameleons
3. telekinesis a. moving of objects by mental power b. broadcasting of films
   c. distant motion d. electronic control from afar
4. hyperkinetic a. overgrown b. large-bodied
   c. intensely active d. projected on a large screen
5. misanthropic a. humanitarian b. wretched c. antisocial d. monumental
6. kinescope a. light meter b. peep show
   c. early movie camera d. camera for live TV

B. Match the definition on the left to the correct word on the right:

1.	protocol	a.	rules of behavior
2.	misanthropic	b.	human-wolf transformation
3.	protagonist	c.	hero or heroine
4.	anthropology	d.	tree-shaped
5.	dendroid	e.	cell contents
6.	protoplasm	f.	study of cultures
7.	lycanthropy	g.	model
8.	prototype	h.	antisocial
9.	anthropoid	i.	ape

C. Fill in each blank with the correct letter:

a. misanthropic   d. protagonist   g. anthropoid
b. protoplasm   e. anthropology   h. protocol
c. lycanthropy   f. prototype

1. The ___ of *The Wizard of Oz* is a Kansas farm girl named Dorothy.
2. According to official ___, the Ambassador from England ranks higher than the Canadian Consul.
3. In the years when new primitive cultures were being discovered regularly, ___ must have been a very exciting field.
4. The gorilla is classified as an ___ because of its relatively close resemblance to humans.
5. There under the microscope we saw the cell's ___ in all its amazing complexity.
6. By the time he turned 80 he was genuinely bitter and ___ and disliked by all his neighbors.
7. The engineers have promised to have the ___ of the new sedan finished by March.
8. In these mountains, where wolves can be heard baying at the moon every night, many of the villagers believe in ___.

D. Complete the analogy:

1. antagonist : villain :: protagonist : ___
   a. maiden b. wizard c. knight d. hero

F. Indicate whether the pairs have the same or different meanings:

1. protocol / rules of behavior   same ___ / different ___
2. rhomboid / shifting shape   same ___ / different ___
3. kinesiology / sports history   same ___ / different ___
4. prototype / model   same ___ / different ___
5. humanoid / manmade   same ___ / different ___
6. kinescope / motion-triggered camera   same ___ / different ___
7. hyperkinetic / overactive   same ___ / different ___
8. dendroid / treelike   same ___ / different ___
9. telekinesis / electronic broadcasting   same ___ / different ___
10. deltoid / shoulder muscle   same ___ / different ___

F. Fill in each blank with the correct letter:

a. anthropology	d. rhomboid	g. prototype
b. humanoid	e. protoplasm	h. deltoid
c. hyperkinetic	f. dendroid	i. erratic

1. Seen from up close, the mosses turn out to be ___, resembling a colony of tiny trees.
2. What he dislikes most about his body is his narrow shoulders, so the first thing he asked his trainer for was some good ___ exercises.
3. Before car makers produce a new model, they always build and test a ___.
4. At 25 he was still as ___ as a 14-year-old, constantly fidgeting at his desk, with his leg bouncing up and down.
5. If life is ever discovered on a distant planet, few scientists expect the life-forms to be ___, even if that's what sci-fi films always show.
6. The jellylike substance in cells is called ___.
7. The antenna takes the shape of a ___, almost a diamond.
8. For his graduate work in ___, he's been doing research on societies in India's tribal areas.
9. The children made only ___ progress because they kept stopping to pick flowers.

UNIT 72

A. Choose the closest definition:

1. fugue   a. mathematical formula   b. musical form   c. marginal figure   d. masonry foundation
2. centrifugal   a. moving upward   b. moving backward   c. moving downward   d. moving outward

3. subterfuge   a. overhead serve   b. underhanded plot
                c. powerful force   d. secret supporter
4. refuge   a. starting point   b. hideout   c. goal   d. return
5. abscond   a. steal   b. discover   c. retire   d. flee

B. Fill in each blank with the correct letter:

a. refuge	d. abstraction	g. subterfuge
b. abscond	e. centrifugal	h. abstruse
c. fugue	f. abstemious	

1. A rock tied to a string and whirled about exerts ____ force on the string.
2. All the plans for the surprise party were in place except the ____ for keeping her out of the house until 6:30.
3. That's a clever ____, but in the real world things work very differently.
4. Fleeing the Nazis, he had found ____ in the barn of a wealthy family in northern Italy.
5. The ____ vocabulary of the literature professor led many students to drop her class.
6. He's given up drinking and leads an ____ life these days, rarely thinking about his former high living.
7. As the last piece in the recital, she had chosen a particularly difficult ____ by Bach.
8. The bride is so shy that her mother fears she'll ____ from the reception.

C. Match the definition on the left to the correct word on the right:

1.	novice	a.	star explosion
2.	neoclassic	b.	new invention or method
3.	abstemious	c.	beginner
4.	innovation	d.	newborn
5.	neoconservative	e.	ancient
6.	abstruse	f.	cleverly new
7.	supernova	g.	favoring aggressive foreign policy
8.	neonatal	h.	resembling Greek and Roman style
9.	abstraction	i.	trick
10.	novel	j.	generalization
11.	Neolithic	k.	flee
12.	subterfuge	l.	difficult
13.	abscond	m.	self-controlled

D. Indicate whether the pairs have the same or different meanings:

1. abstemious / self-controlled   same ___ / different ___
2. abstruse / difficult   same ___ / different ___

E. Fill in each blank with the correct letter:

a. Neolithic   e. neonatal   i. abstruse
b. novice   f. abstraction   j. neoclassic
c. centrifugal   g. supernova   k. innovation
d. novel   h. neoconservative   l. subterfuge

1. My father subscribes to the ___ magazines and still thinks we had no choice but to invade Iraq.
2. The building's style is ___, with Roman columns and with white statues on either side of the entrance.
3. In his youth he had intended to join the priesthood, and he even served as a ___ for six months before giving it up.
4. They're now working at a ___ site in Syria, where they've found evidence of goat, pig, and sheep farming.
5. The baby might not have survived if the hospital hadn't had an excellent ___ ward.
6. The ___ seen by Asian astronomers in 1054 was four times as bright as the brightest planet.
7. The company had a history of ___ that had earned it immense respect and attracted many of the brightest young engineers.
8. She often comes up with ___ interpretations of the evidence in cases like this, and she's sometimes proven correct.
9. He always used to be able to get hold of Grateful Dead tickets by some kind of ___.
10. The researcher's writing was ___ but it was worth the effort to read it.
11. The speech contained one ___ after another, but never a specific example.
12. ___ force keeps roller-coaster cars from crashing to the ground.

UNIT 73

A. Choose the closest definition:

1. geocentric
   a. moonlike b. near earth's core
   c. mathematical d. earth-centered
2. geophysics
   a. physical geometry b. earth science
   c. material science d. science of shapes
3. pyrotechnic
   a. dazzling b. fire-starting c. boiling d. passionate
4. geostationary
   a. polar b. hovering over one location
   c. space-station-related d. equatorial
5. geothermal
   a. globally warmed b. using earth's heat
   c. solar-powered d. tropical

B. Fill in each blank with the correct letter:

a. acrophobic	e. technophile	i. artifice
b. technocrat	f. artifact	j. xenophobe
c. artisan	g. arachnophobia	k. technophobe
d. agoraphobia	h. pyrotechnic	

1. She found a small clay ____ in the shape of a bear at the site of the ancient temple.
2. She still suffers from ____, even though she hasn't had spider nightmares for many years.
3. His ____ is so bad that he won't even accept an award at a ceremony.
4. He used every ____ imaginable to hide his real age from the television cameras.
5. Immigration is almost the only thing he talks about these days, and he seems to have become a full-fledged ____.
6. As governor, he had the reputation of being a ____, convinced that much of the state's problems could be solved by using proper technology and data.
7. The debate between these two remarkable minds was a ____ display of brilliant argument and slashing wit.
8. My father is making a real effort to master e-mail, but my mother is a genuine ____ who just wishes the computer would go away.
9. These beautiful handblown goblets were obviously made by a talented ____.
10. He's so ____ that he had to stay in the car when we visited the Grand Canyon.
11. All through high school and college, computer jocks like him were called nerds or geeks, but he always preferred to be described as a ____.

C. Match the definition on the left to the correct word on the right:

1.	craftsperson	a.	artful
2.	fear of open or public places	b.	xenophobe
3.	ingenious	c.	acrophobic
4.	fear of spiders	d.	artifact
5.	clever skill	e.	artisan
6.	one fearful of foreigners	f.	artifice
7.	man-made object	g.	arachnophobia
8.	fearful of heights	h.	agoraphobia

D. Choose the correct *antonym*:

1. artful   a. lovely   b. sly   c. talented   d. awkward

E. Indicate whether the pairs have the same or different meanings:

1.	acrophobic / fearful of heights	same ____ / different ____
2.	longitude / lines parallel to the equator	same ____ / different ____
3.	technophobe / computer genius	same ____ / different ____
4.	pyrotechnic / spectacular	same ____ / different ____
5.	oblong / unnatural	same ____ / different ____

6. technocrat / mechanic   same ___ / different ___
7. longueur / boring passage   same ___ / different ___
8. technophile / technology hater   same ___ / different ___
9. elongate / stretch   same ___ / different ___
10. technophile / apparatus   same ___ / different ___
11. xenophobe / one fearful of foreigners   same ___ / different ___
12. arachnophobia / fear of spiders   same ___ / different ___

F. Fill in each blank with the correct letter:

a. artful	e. geothermal	i. technocrat
b. geophysics	f. technophobe	j. artifice
c. agoraphobia	g. artifact	k. geocentric
d. artisan	h. geostationary	

1. The strangest ___ they had dug up was a bowl on which an extremely odd animal was painted.
2. Their house is mostly heated by a ___ heat pump, so they pay almost nothing for fuel.
3. Most of us are ___ in our thinking until a grade-school teacher tells us about how the earth revolves around the sun.
4. He'd done an ___ job of writing the proposal so as to appeal to each board member who would have to approve it.
5. Getting a ___ like him to start using a cell phone would be a major achievement.
6. It was the mystery of the earth's magnetic field that eventually led him into the field of ___.
7. Each worker at the tiny textile workshop thought of himself or herself as an ___.
8. The mayor is a ___ who thinks all the city's problems can be fixed by technology and rational management.
9. Each room in the palace was a masterpiece of ___, from its wall paintings to its chandeliers to its delicate furniture.
10. Tens of millions of people couldn't watch TV if it weren't for a fleet of ___ satellites.
11. Her ___ has gotten worse, and now she refuses to even leave the house.

UNIT 74

A. Choose the closest definition:

1. linguistics — a. language study b. reading
   c. mouth surgery d. tongue exercise
2. juncture — a. opening b. crossroads c. end d. combination
3. soliloquy — a. love poem b. monologue c. lullaby d. conversation
4. adjunct — a. warning b. addition c. disclosure d. difference
5. lingua franca — a. Old French b. common language
   c. Italian casserole d. French coin
6. colloquial — a. slangy b. disrespectful c. conversational d. uneducated
7. conjunct — a. joined b. difficult c. spread out d. simplified
8. multilingual — a. highly varied b. in separate parts
   c. born with multiple tongues d. fluent in several languages
9. colloquium — a. field of study b. university
   c. college d. scholarly discussion
10. disjunction — a. prohibition b. break c. requirement d. intersection
11. linguine — a. slang b. pasta c. Italian dessert d. common language
12. loquacious — a. abundant b. silent c. talkative d. informative
13. adjunct — a. addition b. neighbor c. connection d. acquaintance

B. Complete the analogy:

1. tune : melody :: proverb : ____   a. poem b. song c. story d. saying
2. garbage : food :: verbiage : ____   a. boxes b. verbs c. words d. trash
3. relaxed : stiff :: colloquial : ____
   a. conversational b. talkative c. casual d. formal
4. frequently : often :: verbatim : ____
   a. later b. closely c. differently d. exactly
5. sound bite : quotation :: proverb : ____
   a. saying b. sentence c. introduction d. phrase
6. scarce : sparse :: verbose : ____   a. poetic b. wordy c. fictional d. musical

C. Indicate whether the pairs have the same or different meanings:

1. lingua franca / pasta dish   same ___ / different ___
2. colloquial / informal   same ___ / different ___
3. adjunct / supplement   same ___ / different ___
4. linguine / Italian language   same ___ / different ___
5. juncture / train station   same ___ / different ___
6. colloquium / temple   same ___ / different ___
7. disjunction / connection   same ___ / different ___
8. multilingual / using several fingers   same ___ / different ___
9. loquacious / long-winded   same ___ / different ___
10. linguistics / science of singing   same ___ / different ___
11. soliloquy / praise   same ___ / different ___
12. conjunct / split   same ___ / different ___

D. Match the definition on the left to the correct word on the right:

1. adjunct
2. verbiage
3. monologue
4. proverb

a. soliloquy
b. saying
c. wordiness
d. attachment

E. Fill in each blank with the correct letter:

a. lingua franca
b. verbiage
c. disjunction

d. verbatim
e. linguistics
f. proverb

g. colloquium
h. verbose
i. loquacious

1. Please quote me ___ or don't "quote" me at all.
2. He turned out to be a ___ old windbag, and I slept through the whole talk.
3. Most philosophers see no ___ between science and morality.
4. Although he was shy the first time he came to dinner, he's usually downright ___ these days.
5. Unnecessary ___ usually gets in the way of clarity in writing.
6. My professor is participating in the ___, and we're all required to attend.
7. "Nothing ventured, nothing gained" was a favorite ___ of my grandmother's.
8. Never having studied ___, he didn't feel able to discuss word histories in much depth.
9. The Spaniards and Germans at the next table were using English as a ___.

UNIT 75

A. Indicate whether the pairs have the same or different meanings:

1. lucid / glittering — same ___ / different ___
2. photosynthesis / reproduction — same ___ / different ___
3. lumen / lighting — same ___ / different ___
4. elucidate / charm — same ___ / different ___
5. luminary / star — same ___ / different ___
6. translucent / cross-lighted — same ___ / different ___
7. luminous / glowing — same ___ / different ___
8. bioluminescent / brilliant — same ___ / different ___
9. lucubration / nightmare — same ___ / different ___
10. penumbra / half-shadow — same ___ / different ___
11. translucent / light-diffusing — same ___ / different ___
12. photon / elementary particle of light — same ___ / different ___
13. umber / brown — same ___ / different ___

B. Match the definition on the left to the correct word on the right:

1. resentment
2. brownish color
3. clarify
4. passing light but only blurred images
5. elemental particle
6. brightly clear
7. near shadow
8. partially disclose
9. involving the interaction of light with matter
10. production of carbohydrates
11. hard study
12. using light to generate electricity

a. penumbra
b. photoelectric
c. translucent
d. adumbrate
e. photovoltaic
f. umbrage
g. photon
h. umber
i. lucubration
j. elucidate
k. photosynthesis
l. lucid

C. Fill in each blank with the correct letter:

a. photovoltaic
b. lucid
c. photon
d. verbose

e. translucent
f. photoelectric
g. verbatim
h. lucubration

i. photosynthesis
j. elucidate

1. A soft light filtered through the ____ white curtains separating the two rooms.
2. ____ cells on the roof capture the sun's energy, and with the small windmill nearby they produce more energy than the house needs.
3. Few of us can truly imagine that light can be reduced to a tiny packet of energy called a ____.
4. In graduate school, his lively social life was replaced with three years of intense ____.
5. In my afternoon class there's an extremely ____ guy whose "questions" sometimes go on for five minutes.
6. A large tree with a 40-inch trunk may produce two-thirds of a pound of oxygen every day through ____.
7. Since the tape recorder wasn't turned on, there's no ____ record of the meeting.
8. Whenever anyone asks the professor to ____, he just makes everything more complicated instead of less.
9. His 88-year-old aunt is in a nursing home, and he never knows which days she'll be ____.
10. The alarm system depends on ____ technology that detects when someone breaks a beam of light in a doorway.

D. Choose the closest definition:

1. luminary   a. ruler b. lantern c. lighting designer d. celebrity
2. adumbrate   a. revise b. punish c. advertise d. outline

E. Fill in each blank with the correct letter:

a. elucidate	d. luminous	g. umbrage
b. bioluminescent	e. umber	h. luminary
c. penumbra	f. lumen	i. adumbrate

1. All the pigments—crimson, russet, ____, cobalt blue, and the rest—were mixed by his assistants

2. Her ____ voice was all the critics could talk about in their reviews of the musical's opening night.

3. Some people are quick to take ____ the moment they think someone might have been disrespectful.

4. The ____ insects that he studies use their light for mating.

5. The light output of an ordinary candle provided the basis for the light unit called the ____ .

6. The farther away a source of light is from the object casting a shadow, the wider will be that shadow's ____.

7. The book's introduction helps ____ how the reader can make the best use of it.

8. The increasing cloudiness and the damp wind seemed to ____ a stormy night.

9. He had just been introduced to another ____ of the literary world and was feeling rather dazzled.

A. 1.d 2.d 3.f 4.d 5.s 6.d 7.s 8.d 9.d 10.s 11.s 12.e 13.s B. 1.f 2.h 3.j 4.c 5.g 6.j 7.a 8.d 9.b 10.f 11.j 12.e C. 1.e 2.a 3.c 4.h 5.d 6.j 7.g 8.j 9.b 10.f D. 1.d 2.d E. 1.e 2.d 3.g 4.b 5.f 6.c 7.a 8.j 9.h

미리엄웹스터 보캐뷸러리 빌더 워크북

초판 1쇄 발행 2020년 1월 31일
초판 2쇄 인쇄 2022년 2월 2일

지은이 Mary Wood Cornog
옮긴이 크레센도 번역가집단
꾸민이 김정환
펴낸이 윤영삼
펴낸곳 콘체르토
주소 서울 강서구 마곡중앙로 171, 프라이빗타워2차 511호
전화 070-8688-6616
팩스 0303-3441-6616
전자우편 editor@xcendo.net
홈페이지 xcendo.net
트위터 twitter.com/xcendo
페이스북 facebook.com/bookbeez
Copyright ⓒ 콘체르토 2020, Seoul
ISBN 979-11-965472-2-6 [13740]

이 책에 관한 더 많은 자료를 얻고 싶다면
QR코드를 스캔하세요.
[xcendo.net/voca로 연결됩니다.]

이 책은 2020년 콘체르토에서 출간한 **미리엄웹스터 보캐뷸러리빌더** 한국어판의 별책부록입니다